The Mind On Edge

An Introduction to John Jay Chapman's
Philosophy of Higher Education

Including Chapman's principal writings on colleges

Alan L. Contreras

Our Universities copyright Columbia University Press
reprinted with permission.

ISBN 978-0-9893848-0-3

CRANEDANCE PUBLICATIONS
PO BOX 50535, Eugene, OR 97405
541-345-3974

The Mind On Edge

"He just looks at things, and tells the truth about them—a strange thing even to *try* to do…"

— William James, on John Jay Chapman

Contents

Note: *Our Universities* is reprinted by arrangement with Columbia University Press.

An Introduction to John Jay Chapman

John Jay Chapman (1862-1933) was one of the greatest essayists that the United States ever produced, but his work is remarkably unnoticed today. Many people whose philosophical outlook is congruent with his, or who would greatly appreciate his work, don't even recognize his name, let alone have any familiarity with his work.

Over the years he has had several high-profile promoters, including William James, Edmund Wilson, Jacques Barzun and, with reservations, Alfred Kazin. He is surely among few essayists who inspired a significant poem, Muriel Rukeyser's "Chapman."[1] Yet for some reason his work, reasonably well-known in his own lifetime, has failed to "take" with modern American readers. Even Wikipedia, which sometimes slathers acres of text on lesser-known figures, gives him an extremely modest and incomplete entry.[2]

This is true in spite of the fact that much of his writing is not only brilliantly conceived and spectacularly written, but remarkably applicable to issues that we deal with today. His 1898 essay "Politics," an exposition on how a large business comes to dominate a town, remains a splendid expression of political insight—it would be a perfect college-class garnish to a classic work such as Robert Dahl's *Who Governs?* or any more recent similar work—and many of his political writings during the Gilded Age and

---

[1] Muriel Rukeyser, "Chapman," in *A Turning Wind* (1939). For a discussion of this poem in the context of Rukeyser's poetry, see Aisha Ravindran, Intuiting Reality: the Poetry of Muriel Rukeyser. 2002. Ph.D. Thesis, Mahatma Gandhi University, India.

[2] Accessed April 25, 2012.

the early 20ᵗʰ Century remain among the best writing ever done on American politics.

His essay "Between Elections" (1890) is certainly worthy of much greater discussion in political science classes, and is a natural mate with "Politics," which the editors of the 1998 collection of his works recognized. I suspect that the fact that these essays are fairly short and have not been cited often enough to make them "academic" is a factor in their lack of status.

Chapman's address "Coatesville," on a lynching in Pennsylvania, is, of course, a unique piece of Americana and represents the best of the American spirit. I say "of course" because I would think that most Americans interested in their nation's history would have come across it and kept it in their short list of great events. It deserves a place in any "best of" collection on American political commentary. Unfortunately the compilers of such things do not realize this.

We owe to a small number of dedicated enthusiasts the fact that much of Chapman's writing, including all of his major work, remains findable, if not technically in print. The extraordinary *Collected Works of John Jay Chapman*[3] is a twelve-volume gold mine that includes his twenty-six major publications and the entirety of his political magazine in a well-produced, easily readable facsimile form. The format retains original pagination, which is helpful to researchers. It is still available, but only by direct contact with the publisher.

Two volumes of selected works have appeared, one edited by Barzun in 1957[4] and one edited by Richard Stone

---

[3] Melvin Bernstein, ed., *Collected Works of John Jay Chapman*, (Massachusetts: M&S Press [currently Rhode Island], 1970).

[4] Jacques Barzun, ed., *The Selected Writings of John Jay Chapman*, (New York: Farrar, Straus, 1957).

in 1998.[5] These include some material not in the *Collected Works* because it never appeared in book form; unfortunately both are out of print, though easily located through book search services such as ABE online. Some of his original work is also available through used book dealers.

William James, whose epigraph about Chapman's truth-telling [6] appears at the beginning of this book, referred to Chapman's writing style as "all splinters,"[7] which is a reasonable way of looking at the irresistible avalanche of short, crisp, punchy sentences that fill most of his work. Spiky, incisive, pointed, edgy and by all means penetrating describe them well.

His work, taken as a whole, generates quite various responses as to its quality and value. Edmund Wilson wrote that Chapman was "our best writer on literature of his generation—who made the Babbitts and the Mores and the Brownells, for all the more formidable rigor of their systems and the bulkier mass of their work, look like colonial schoolmasters." [8] Yet Alfred Kazin, though appreciating Chapman's intellect and power, considered him not "professional" and said that he "never did a book that was a solid contribution to the subject" and spent too much time building his own myth.[9]

---

[5] Richard Stone, ed., *Unbought Spirit: A John Jay Chapman Reader*, (Champaign: Illinois, 1998).

[6] The epigraph about Chapman's looking at things and telling the truth about them appeared in a letter from James to Frances R. Morse on April 12, 1900. The letter appears in *The Selected Letters of William James*, ed. Elizabeth Hardwick (Boston: Godine, 1980), 184.

[7] William James to George H. Palmer, April 2, 1900, in *The Selected Letters*, 181.

[8] Edmund Wilson, *The Triple Thinkers* (New York: Oxford University Press, 1948), 141.

[9] Alfred Kazin, *Contemporaries* (Boston: Little, Brown; 1959), 68.

4

Both of these views can be true in context. Certainly Chapman's essays on higher education, the focus of the current volume, are a solid contribution to the subject, because the subject, as he approaches it, does not require research, but rather a clear eye, a perceptive mind and an accurate pen. Chapman had these in abundance. They are, in effect, philosophy, not science, and the distinction is one that was very significant in Chapman's own mind.

In later years, Chapman tended to issue more ill-considered comments, including miscellaneous anti-Semitic and anti-Catholic noises. Edmund Wilson wrote perceptively of this period that "one is made more and more uncomfortable by the feeling that one has been shut up in a chamber from which the air is being gradually withdrawn—shut in with a chafing spirit who, baffled of finding an outlet, is sometimes furious and sometimes faint."[10]

In addition to the *Collected Works* and the two volumes of selected essays, there are additional major works on Chapman. Mark A. DeWolfe Howe issued a hybrid biography and large selection of letters in 1937.[11] Bernstein himself wrote a short biography (with an excellent chapter on Chapman's views of education) in 1964.[12] A longer biography by Richard Hovey appeared in 1959.[13] Owen Wister published a remembrance.[14]

Finally, a modern biography by Christoph Irmscher is in process. That is very good news for those of us who

---

[10] *The Triple Thinkers*, 162.

[11] Mark A. DeWolfe Howe, *John Jay Chapman and his Letters*, (Boston: Houghton Mifflin, 1937).

[12] Melvin Bernstein, *John Jay Chapman*, (New York: Twayne, 1964).

[13] Richard Hovey, *John Jay Chapman, an American Mind*, (New York: Columbia, 1959).

[14] Owen Wister, *Two Appreciations*, privately printed by The Marchbanks Press (1934).

recognize that Chapman is worthy of continued study and reflection.

Chapman has had occasional attention in articles, dissertations and other academic works; in this book I cite only those that relate to his views on higher education, unless there is a special reason to include such a reference.

A note on style and format

For convenience, Chapman is often referred to as JJC in the notes. Certain principal references, e.g. his own books and the letters of William James, are referred to in short form after the initial citation.

Chapman's View of Higher Education

This book concentrates on what Chapman had to say about colleges and college-level education. He also wrote extensively about "schools" and education in general, but that writing tends to be intermingled with his discussions of other subjects, particularly art and the fine arts in general. There are hundreds of such references in scores of venues. Thus I have chosen to leave largely untouched his writing on what we would today in the United States call "K-12" education. Much of it is available in the *Collected Works*. In its general theme of attention to the classics and the primacy of original unmediated sources, it follows his views on higher education.

Melvin Bernstein, editor of the *Collected Works*, commented that Chapman thought "the grand design of education was to pulverize dogma and destroy its constricting powers."[15] That is as good a place to start as any. Another way of putting it is that Chapman considered his own way of grabbing an issue by the throat and flailing away at it until it was dealt with to be the way that any thinking person should behave.

Thus colleges should not support or encourage any kind of faint-heartedness and should in fact support educating students in the finest points of their tradition and culture so that they could, upon entering society, proceed to attack anything that was going bad.

Chapman's philosophy of higher education (and everything else) has three basic themes that individually and in combination underlie almost all of his positions. These themes are:

---

[15] Introduction to Vol. 3 of the *Collected Works*.

Dislike of hierarchies. He saw no reason why he should not have a personal relationship with God, and if he had one with God, then why not with everyone else?

Dislike of intermediaries. He had a strong preference for experiencing all of life first-hand.

Dislike of the abuse of systems that should in theory make life better. This was especially clear in his writing on governments and churches.

These three basics appear many times in his writing on college education. We see them with particular clarity in his writing on (and attitude toward) the classics, his mixed feelings about the role of science and business and his remarkably understated views on the connection of religion and higher education.

I have ordered my comments into five sections that correspond to the fundamental pillars of Chapman's outlook on education. These segments are as follows:

The Classical Base
Religious Underpinnings
The Relationship of Colleges to Business
The Limits of Science
The Nature of Academic Excellence

My comments are simply an introduction and outline to Chapman's work. When you read his complete essays, you will come to appreciate that any 'summary' necessarily ignores the fact that almost all of Chapman's sentences are memorable: I could obtain fiery quotes or analytical mileage out of almost every one. Rather than allow my own words to obscure his, I will offer only basic commentaries and encourage you to follow his own precept that a reader should engage with an author directly. He was perfectly at home arguing with the ghosts of writers dead two thousand years; may you feel similarly at home with his work.

The Classical Base

Chapman's insistence on the value of the Classics, particularly the Greeks, strikes us today as a splendid archaism. Who, after all, translates Greek drama essentially for pleasure today, as Chapman did in great swathes? Alfred Kazin considered these translations almost an affront to scholarship, calling this aspect of Chapman's life work "presumptuous"[16] and harrumphing that such work should only be done by professionals, which in his view Chapman was not. Edmund Wilson had a more sanguine view, noting that Chapman often saw things that others had missed owing to his unique way of treating ancient authors as though they were his next-door neighbors over for a barbecue.[17]

Chapman's view was never more clearly put, nor less equivocal, than in this statement:

> Drop the classics from education? Ask rather, Why not drop education? For the classics are education. We cannot draw a line and say, 'Here we start.' The facts are the other way. We started long ago, and our very life depends upon keeping alive all that we have thought and felt during our history. If the continuity is taken from us, we shall relapse.
>
> The survival of Greek literature civilized the Romans, and the Revival of Learning transformed the mind of modern Europe. You will say that it is a strange thing

---

[16] Alfred Kazin, *Contemporaries*, p. 57.

[17] Both Kazin's brief and slightly sour appreciation in *Contemporaries* and Wilson's much longer and more detailed account in *The Triple Thinkers* are worth reading on the subject of how Chapman fit into his world, and Wilson in particular on his relationship to classical literature. Neither says much about his views on education, which have been largely ignored by commentators, except for Bernstein.

that man should advance by looking backward, yet it seems to be a fact that literature and the fine arts have always been the outcome of man's endeavor to reconstruct an imaginary past. We sit, as it were, with our backs to the driver and can only deal with what we see, or think we see, in the past. Any acquaintance with the past fertilizes our minds. This assumption has always been taken as the basis of all education. It is the corner stone on which every school and university in the world has been founded. The notion that we belong to the future seems to sterilize a man—as may be seen in those recent attempts in painting, poetry and music in which the author consciously endeavors to separate himself from the past. The future is a cold mystery, the past is warm with life. [18]

When we think of the Classics at all, it is the occasional aphorism or misquoting politician that comes to mind, not the full-scale immersion that was the basis of a liberal education in the 19th Century and still very much alive in the early 20th Century. Even Alfred North Whitehead, writing in 1929, said that

No more deadly harm can be done to young minds than by depreciation of the present. The present contains all that there is. It is holy ground; for it is the past, and it is the future.[19]

Chapman was profoundly connected to the literary past even as he was vigorously connected to the political present. Even as Edmund Wilson expressed his frustration with Chapman's errors and unprofessional disconnection from the norms of academic discourse, he noted that:

---

[18] From *Our Universities* (1932).

[19] Alfred North Whitehead, *The Aims of Education and other essays*. Free Press, 1967 (1929).

To Chapman, the great writers of the past were neither a pantheon or a vested interest. He approached them open-mindedly and boldly, very much as he did living persons who he thought might entertain or instruct him.

…

To me, Chapman's flashlighting and spotlighting in his studies of the Greeks, Dante, Shakespeare and Goethe are among the few real recent contributions to the knowledge of these familiar subjects. He cannot help bumping into aspects which, though they bulk very large in these authors, have so often been ignored or evaded that many people have never noticed they were there.[20]

In essence, Chapman derived his values and ways of thought from many centuries past and applied them to modern problems of his era, whether they were suitable or not. With a few exceptions, he skipped over the two hundred years prior to his birth as a source for inspiration. This "bridging" effect appears frequently in his writing, for example this statement of basic values:

It is in vain that you argue with one of our university managers that the aim of a university is to connect the mind of the student with the thought of the ages. He wishes to prepare the student for the life of the day.[21]

Even when he looks at a modern author (from his vantage, Shakespeare was almost contemporary), his focus is always on the ancient connections:

---

[20] Edmund Wilson, *The Triple Thinkers*, p. 157.
[21] From *Our Universities* (1932).

> We think of Shakespeare as of a lightly-lettered person; but he was ransacking books all day to find plots and language for his plays. He reeks with mythology, he swims in classical metaphor: and, if he knew the Latin poets only in translation, he knew them with that famished intensity of interest which can draw the meaning through the walls of a bad text. Deprive Shakespeare of his sources, and he could not have been Shakespeare.
>
> ...
>
> Shakespeare borrowed this speech [of Prospero] from Medea's speech in Ovid, which he knew in the translation of Arthur Golding; and really Shakespeare seems almost to have held the book in his hand while penning Prospero's speech.[22]

Chapman's view of the progress of knowledge was a paean to recycling: he apparently considered there to be a finite number of ideas and artistic forms and expressions available, and described our creative efforts thus:

> There is, and is to be, no end of this reappearance of old metapor [sic], old trade secret, old usage of art. No sooner has a masterpiece appeared, that summarizes all knowledge, than men get up eagerly the next morning with chisel and brush, and try again. Nothing done satisfies. It is all in the making that the inspiration lies; and this endeavor renews itself with the ages, and grows by devouring its own offspring [23]

We can read with a smile his idea about how a boy (there were no girls in his vision of college) of promise would end up in college:

---

[22] From *Learning* (1910).
[23] From *Learning* (1910).

Meanwhile there is probably not a high school in the land that does not contain one or two boys who are fitted by nature and disposition for a life of scholarship. A youth of this sort ought to walk home with the master after class, and on passing to the university, should carry a line of introduction to the head of its Latin department. You smile. It is nevertheless worth while to consider things that seem to be impossible, for they sometimes give the key to the future. That a boy should walk home with his teacher involves the infiltration of a new spirit into our education and the general acceptance of a very simple truth which to the American mind seems incomprehensible—namely, that education is not baggage but power.[24]

He anticipates our tolerant smile and our willingness to pass over his quaint notions,[25] but he also states with prescient clarity our very modern recognition that knowledge is power. This is one of the enigmas of Chapman: his clear recognition of the value of knowledge in society melded with a disdain for, or lack of awareness of, how the pathways to power had changed during his lifetime. He remained planted socially in 1895 and intellectually in 476. The knowledge necessary to operate effectively in the expanding world of science and business represented to Chapman a kind of infestation of education by foreign agents rather than an expansion of knowledge. I discuss this more in the chapters on science and business.

---

[24] From *Our Universities* (1932).

[25] One thing Chapman did not anticipate is the depersonalization of the educational relationship. Any teacher who took a student home with him, even once, would be treated today as a probable criminal and at a very minimum admonished never to do so again, if indeed he wasn't fired.

To conclude this brief look at Chapman's connection to the classical world let us look at his wistful notions of how modern colleges might connect to Greek culture:

> Our colleges have become, as it were, the racing-stables of competing millionaires, and the whole movement of university-building has become a kind of national sport. But one cannot say that this is an unmixed evil. There is an ethical element in sport. The competing merchants of Athens paid enormous sums for the staging of the tragedies of Aeschylus and Sophocles. Our colleges are today constantly reviving Greek plays, and their graduates present them with stadia and open-air theaters. Tomorrow these same benefactors may subscribe to raise the salary of the Greek professor. The present age is so sensitively organized that a sincere revival of scholarship in any small college would be felt and reflected everywhere. All depends on what shall go forward in the breasts of the American people outside of the universities.[26]

---

[26] From *Our Universities* (1932). We cannot expect any rising interest in Greek theater in the breasts of the American people anytime soon.

Religious Underpinnings

William James wrote to Chapman that "No one touches certain deep moral truths as you do."[27] Anyone reading much of Chapman cannot help but conclude that a goal of stating moral truths was at the core of almost everything he wrote. Saved from stridency (except for some occasional bellowing at the Catholic Church) by the same light touch and sense of humor that undoubtedly kept some academics from taking him seriously, his moralizing came clothed in so many forms that it never seemed threatening, at least in a religious sense. It was so much a core part of his person that no one could possibly mistake it for something put on for show or effect, unlike some other aspects of Chapman's always-entertaining tale-telling.

His educational philosophy was profoundly affected by the idea that colleges exist in order to convey to the young certain moral and philosophical values previously discovered by or revealed to their elders. However, he did not, in his educational writings, comment in much detail on just what the religious basis for his thoughts was. This may be because his faith was such a basic part of his life that he felt no need to mention it.

However, he wrote extensively on religion in two books and the subject pops up elsewhere as well.[28] He was completely at home both supporting the necessity of Biblical knowledge and deprecating religion gone bad. I suspect that at least part of the answer lies in his dislike of hierarchies and compulsions.

---

27 William James to JJC, May 18, 1906, in *The Selected Letters*, 225.

28 See in particular *Notes on Religion* (1915) and *Letters and Religion* (1924), reprinted together as vol. 11 of the *Collected Works*.

His dislike for the power structure and operational norms of the Catholic church was simply the pinnacle of a fairly sizable pyramid: there was no room in his philosophy for organized religion of any kind if the result was the establishment of a screen or barrier between the individual and God. His peculiar relationship with Judaism appears to have represented a respect for its traditions and lack of intercessory impedimenta combined with a dislike of individual Jews and the fact that he may have connected Judaism with the excessively grasping American business culture that he detested.

His 'normal' relationship with Protestantism seems to have been rooted in those aspects that allowed direct interpersonal connections with God. If we were to take C.E.S. Wood's contemporaneous satire *Heavenly Discourse*[29] but treat it as a perfectly accurate record of conversations between God and various people, we would have an approximation of how Chapman might have imagined his communications with the Almighty. Not so casual as "Hey God, how's it going," but certainly a pretty ordinary conversation.

His views could be and often were set forth with a vigor, directness and clarity that could surprise and even shock recipients. His friends got exactly the same "treatment" as his opponents: when your moral goal is to tell all the truth all the time, it is impious to offer different versions to different audiences. As William James noted in a response to one of Chapman's letters, "A certain witness at a poisoning case was asked how the corpse looked. 'Pleasant-like and foaming at the mouth,' was the reply. A

---

[29] Charles Erskine Scott Wood, *Heavenly Discourse* (1927). This is a hilarious look at how heaven might operate and what God's daily problems really are.

good description of you, describing philosophy, in your letter."[30]

This is the unique communicative style of Chapman: polite, even humorous, but so filled with perfectly constructed, impeccably aimed darts and arrows of raw truth that one might as well call them guided missives. He knew perfectly well what his style felt like, but he considered it the way *everyone* should communicate. In *Between Elections* he says that "Everyone in America is soft, and hates conflict. The cure for this, both in politics and social life, is the same,—hardihood. Give them raw truth. They think they will die."[31]

I suspect that the reason we don't see much direct discussion of religion in his works on higher education is that his strong dislike of intervening authority in education combined with the same feeling about religion, or perhaps I should say faith, led him to abjure anything compulsory about the way religion would be made part of a curriculum.

---

[30] William James to JJC, April 30, 1909, in *The Selected Letters*, 254.

[31] JJC, "Between Elections," from *Practical Agitation*, p. 49. Included in *Collected Works* Vol 2.

The Relationship of Colleges to Business

Chapman loathed the interference of business with the work of universities. This intense dislike related to almost any connection between the private, outside world of commerce and what he considered the properly insular function of college education. Not only did he dislike such external connections, but he didn't think universities should even employ people who thought like businessmen did, except perhaps an accountant or two kept safely on a tether somewhere, preferaby not visible to the "pure" academics who ought to be doing everything else at the college.

He had this view in common with British philosopher Michael Oakeshott, generally considered a conservative, whose view of the connection between business and college was summed up in the following statement:

> "[Such things as advanced training]…belong to a world of power and utility, of exploitation, of social and individual egoism, and of activity, whose meaning lies outside itself in some trivial result or achievement—and this is not the world to which a university belongs; it is not the world to which education in the true sense belongs. It is a very powerful world; it is wealthy, interfering and well-meaning. But it is not remarkably self-critical; it is apt to mistake itself for the whole world, and with amiable carelessness it assumes that whatever does not contribute to its own purposes is somehow errant. A university needs to beware of the patronage of this world, or it will find that it has sold its birthright for a mess of pottage…"[32]

---

[32] Michael Oakeshott, *The Voice of Liberal Learning*, page 103.

Oakeshott's view is supported by Anglo-American journalist Andrew Sullivan, whose own conservatism also takes a non-mercantile view of higher education:

> "Education, itself, if reduced to the purpose of 'training' or 'socializing' citizens for a particular end or 'common good' is anathema both to human autonomy and to the correct understanding of education itself...."[33]

Thus Chapman's doubts about this connection remain alive today in the minds of major thinkers and writers.

To a certain extent Chapman conflated business with many aspects of science, another commonality with Oakeshott, who considered science to have little to do with critical thinking, and to be primarily an offshoot of engineering and other applied occupations. A good summary of Chapman's attitude is the following:

> There are, then, in the modern world these two influences which are hostile to education,—the influence of business and the influence of uninspired science. In Europe these influences are qualified by the vigor of the old learning. In America they dominate remorselessly, and make the path of education doubly hard.
>
> ...
>
> Commerce has been our ruler for many years; and yet it is only quite recently that the philosophy of commerce can be seen in our colleges. The business man is not a monster; but he is a person who desires to advance his own interests. This is his occupation and, as it were, his religion. The advancement of material interests constitutes civilization to him. He unconsciously

---

infuses the ideas and methods of business into anything that he touches. It has thus come about in America that our universities are beginning to be run as business colleges. They advertise, they compete with each other, they pretend to give good value to their customers. They desire to increase their trade, they offer social advantages and business openings to their patrons. [34]

In theory, society provides *education* in order to allow people to better pursue their own goals and interests as they see fit. We have *training* in order to help people better pursue other people's goals and interests as they see fit. [35] These are both legitimate purposes, but they are not the same—or at least not until recently, when training has all but eaten education as a societal goal.

We who today hear calls for college accountability and program utility at ever hand, and doubt some aspects of the underlying premise, can enjoy Chapman's views:

If education is to break down as a commercial asset, what excuse have they for retaining it at all ? They will force the colleges to live up to the advertisements and to furnish the kind of education that pays its way. It is clear that if the colleges persist in the utilitarian view, the higher learning will disappear.

In the past the tyrannies have been political tyrannies, and these have become well understood through the struggles of intellect in the past; but the present commercial tyranny is a new thing and as yet little understood. It lies like a heavy fog of intellectual

---

[34] From *Learning* (1910).

[35] For a more extensive discussion of this dichotomy, see David Noble, *Digital Diploma Mills* (2002). People can, of course, pursue training out of purely personal interest, for example, in craft work, geographic information systems, photography, cooking or other fields.

depression over the whole kingdom of Mammon, and is fed by the smoke from a million factories.[36]

His disdain for college leaders, as distinguished from the faculty—or at least the faculty in fields that he liked—is well stated in this comment:

> In America, society has been reorganized since 1870; the old universities have been totally changed and many new ones founded. The money to do this has come from the business world. The men chosen to do the work have been chosen by the business world. Of a truth, it must needs be that offenses come; but woe be unto him through whom the offense cometh. As the Boss has been the tool of the business man in politics, so the College president has been his agent in education. The colleges during this epoch have each had a "policy" and a directorate. They have been manned and commissioned for a certain kind of service, as you might man a fishing-smack to catch herring. [37]

I find his assessment of the nature of college presidents to be quite applicable to the modern era, an era in which the highest career goal of any such president appears to be the avoidance of controversy.

> The men who, during this era, have been chosen to become college presidents have, as a rule, begun life with the ambition of scholars; but their talents for affairs have been developed at the expense of their taste for learning, and they have become hard men. As toward their faculties they have been autocrats, because the age has demanded autocracy here; as toward the

---

[36] From *Learning* (1910).
[37] From *Professorial Ethics* (1910).

millionaire they have been sycophants, because the age
has demanded sycophancy here.

...

The millionaire and the college president are simply
middle men, who transmit the pressure from the
average citizen to the learned classes. What the average
citizen desires to have done in education gets itself
accomplished, though the process should involve the
extinction of the race of educated gentlemen. [38]

Finally, Chapman thinks that a revolt of scholars would
shame college leaders into doing the right thing by true
learning. Although at first glance this idea seems fanciful,
it is not far off what happened in 2012 when the trustees
of the University of Virginia engaged in a ham-fisted
attempt to ditch a president whose patterns of thought
were not the same as those of the wealthy business people
on the board.

> ... the scholars should take the public into their
> confidence and dominate the business men on our
> college boards. This will be found more easy than at
> first appears, because the money element, the
> millionaire element, is very sensitive to public feeling,
> and once the millionaire succumbs, the college
> president will succumb also. The step beyond this
> would consist in the scholars' taking charge of the
> college themselves, merely making use of certain
> business men on their boards for purposes of financial
> administration.[39]

Despite his notion that colleges could be decoupled from
inappropriate oversight by businessmen, he recognized

---

[38] From *Professorial Ethics* (1910).
[39] From *Professorial Ethics* (1910).

that part of the problem was a change in the way students thought about their college experience:

> Is it not clear that the administrators of our colleges merely exhibit one variety of money-madness and their students another? How can one hope to reform or civilize either of those elements, the administrators who are afflicted with a mania for grandeur or the boys in their charge who feel Business in their blood,— Business, as it were, the Call of the Wild? [40]

There is also a grudging but honest recognition that what was happening in higher education represented the best of American energy and creativity, even though coupled to goals that he considered wrongheaded:

> The startling transformation of our old, somnolent halls or shanties of learning into gigantic factories of business men, which took place between 1870 and 1900, is a credit to the public spirit of our leading citizens. But it came about so suddenly and involved so much building, planning and operating that our benefactors and their subordinates, the college authorities, forgot that any kind of talent except business talent was required in the conduct of a university. The transformation was governed by the thought of the whole American people. Science was adopted as their dogma, and the manuals of science as their prayer books. Science took the place which Dogma once held in the medieval universities; and Business, the daughter of Science, was given the niche in the rotunda once filled by Theology. [41]

---

[40] From *The New Dawn in Education* (1926).
[41] From *Our Universities* (1932).

This is as good a point as any from which to depart for the most important and complex of Chapman's arguments with the modern age, that of the role of science.

The Limits of Science

Even in the world of science, which Chapman viewed with qualified suspicion much as Michael Oakeshott did later in the 20th Century, Chapman insisted that the closer science got to what he perceived as fundamentals, the more it would enter the world of the ancients and be compelled to speak in classical terms:

> No matter how revolutionary scientific thought may be, it must resort to metaphysics when it begins to formulate its ultimate meanings. Now when you approach metaphysics, the Greek and the Hebrew have been there before you- are very near to matters which you never intended to approach. You are back at the beginning of all things, human thought does not advance, it only recurs.
>
> … Surely, the Latin classics are as valuable a deposit as the crustacean fossils, or the implements of the Stone Age. When science shall have assumed her true relation to the field of human culture we shall all be happier. To-day science knows that the silkworm must be fed on the leaves of the mulberry tree but does not know that the soul of man must be fed on the Bible and the Greek classics. Science knows that a queen bee can be produced by care and feeding, but does not as yet know that every man who has had a little Greek and Latin in his youth belongs to a different species from the ignorant man. No matter how little it may have been, it reclassifies him. There is more kinship between that man and a great scholar than there is between the same man and some one who has had no classics at all: he breathes from a different part of his anatomy. [42]

---

42 From *Learning* (1910).

Chapman was a notable critic of excessive deference to science in college education. To him, science respected only what was in its own "shop window." Yet as the nation changes, our economy and public dialogue are increasingly infused with talk of science. Science informs us of the decline of the Spotted Owl, provides the life history of wild vs. hatchery salmon and announces new genetically engineered crops. We ask science to predict the behavior of volcanoes, storms, cougars, asteroids and people. Our universities are classified by bureaucrats in significant part on how well they conduct scientific work, and on what scale. The concept of quality in a university setting has become increasingly rooted in scientific accomplishment.

This recognition of the centrality of science is laudable, but there is a risk in asking of science that which it is not capable of providing. That, I think, is what concerned Chapman. Even as we pluck the fruits of science in some fields, we become reluctant listeners when science tells us things we don't want to hear.

Although science can tell us what is true; it cannot tell us what is good. For help with that decision we must look elsewhere, and it is this other arena—that of civic morality and ethics—that needs the greatest attention in the coming decades. It is that package of moral and ethical issues that Chapman thought should be the basis of a genuine college education.

Science is a small word that embraces a large field of human activity. Paul Valéry wrote that "...verifiable evidence...is the exact meaning of the word scientific,"[43] which is as good a way as any of planting the fence, with some activities (e.g. religion) compelled to remain outside and others belonging inside. It covers everything from

---

[43] Paul Valéry, *The Outlook for Intelligence*, p. 103 (Bollingen 1962).

studying invisible particles slung at high speeds by accelerators to evaluating processes so large and inclusive that they encompass more than our entire planet.

All of these have one thing in common: a certain process broadly known as scientific method, which differs from the methods of the fine arts, thus:

> The chief difference between science and art is this, that the statements and conclusions of science can be verified. They all depend upon measurements and calculations on which all the professional scientists of the world agree. But as to music and painting and poetry, the meanings and messages they bring differ with each listener or observer or reader. A second difference is that science comes to stay because it is a utility. It is a constant and cumulative possession. The ages of art pass like clouds: they cannot be arrested.[44]

Chapman's concern was multilinear: he worried about the net impact on society of the "mechanical" age and its overwhelming noise, speed and distraction, he recognized that there is daily practical value in science, he did not like the supercession of science over the humanities in universities and he deprecated the effect of higher education refocusing on *mass* needs and away from the classics and humanities, which is related to his concern about scientific hegemony but not the same thing.

Science became the preeminent academic sphere in the last half of the 20th century, and the consequences have been mixed. Chapman saw this coming and warned against it:

> To begin with, we must find fault with the Brotherhood of Science on much the same ground that

---

[44] From *Our Universities* (1932).

we fought the old religions, grounds of tyranny and narrowness, and presumption. In the next place, it is evident that, in so far as science is not hallowed by the spirit of religion, it is a mere extension of business. It is the essence of world-business, race-business, cosmic-business. It saves time, saves lives, and dominates the air and the sea; but all these things may be accomplished, for ought we know, in the course of the extinction of the better nature of mankind. Science is not directly interested in expression of spiritual truth; her notation cannot include anything so fluctuating, so indeterminate, as the language of feeling. Science neither sings nor jokes; neither prays nor rejoices; neither loves nor hates. This is not her fault; but her limitation. Her fault is that, as a rule, she respects only her own language and puts trust only in what is in her own shop window.

I deprecate the contempt which science expresses for anything that does not happen to be called science. Imperial and haughty science proclaims its occupancy of the whole province of human thought; yet, as a matter of fact, science deals in a language of its own, in a set of formulae and conceptions which cannot cover the most important interests of humanity. It does not understand the value of the fine arts and is always at loggerheads with philosophy. Is it not clear that science, in order to make good her claim to universality, must adopt a conception of her own function that shall leave to the fine arts and to religion their languages? She cannot hope to compete with these languages, nor to translate or expound them. She must accept them. At present she tramples upon them.[45]

Does she still trample upon them? Science brought us penicillin, machine guns, aircraft and mustard gas at about

---

[45] From *Learning* (1910).

the same time, considering the length of human history. Likewise the advent of sulfa, nuclear weapons, polio vaccine and "research" on human subjects in concentration camps. Thus we can see in the century just passed below the horizon both the positive and negative uses of scientific advances. I think Chapman's concerns were overstated, but there are certainly times and circumstances in which the lack of a moral umbrella over actions that scientific advances have made possible is cause for concern.

The visibility and influence of science in our society has become so great that merely labeling something "science" makes an otherwise dull enterprise seem modern, exciting, important, truthful and, perhaps most important, lucrative. Things that are not science are seen by some as unnecessary and probably wasteful. Robert Maynard Hutchins noted that

> "The reverence that science has inspired has led scholars in other disciplines, seeking equally notable results and equally high prestige, to apply the method of science to subject matters to which it is not appropriate. Only trivial results can be accomplished by these means. Science has trivialized other fields of learning."[46]

The word "science" is a magnet and a legitimizing device for departments that feel left behind as technical fields soak up grant money and universities redefine their mission to become trainers for specific workplace roles. Robert Grudin, professor emeritus at the University of Oregon, reminds us that:

---

[46] Robert Maynard Hutchins, *The University of Utopia*, p. 15 (2nd Ed., 1964).

> "specialized excellence has two dangers: that we will
> use it as a means of ignoring our own weak areas, and
> that specialized society will offer us excessive rewards
> for it, yoking us to plow a thin furrow."[47]

Modern specialized science gives people more toys
and improves our efficiency. Medical knowledge has
certainly benefited from science, as has knowledge of the
natural world. These are laudable goals, but not the only
goals. By themselves they do not make a better society or
give people better lives, except in their narrow areas of
specialization. Chapman states the problem thus:

> Science is today the popular language that is drawing
> the world together, and many people think that it is
> taking up the mission of the old humanities: the two
> are often mingled together in the public mind. But the
> two Empires of Science and the Humanities are in
> truth governed by two different kinds of force. The
> first is automatic and is recorded and manipulated by
> instruments and mathematical calculations. The second
> is personal and is recorded in aesthetic and philosophic
> symbols and traditions. Science cannot say a kind word,
> make a joke or turn a tune. Science has neither heart,
> lungs, body, taste nor feeling. It detects what the eye
> cannot see and records what the ear cannot hear. It
> transmits man's various voices, but has no voice of its
> own. It is more silent than the sphinx.[48]

> It is hard to explain the value of education to men who
> have forgotten the meaning of education: its symbols
> convey nothing to them.

---

[47] Robert Grudin, *The Grace of Great Things*, p. 33 (1990).
[48] From *Our Universities* (1932).

The situation is very similar in dealing with scientific men,—at least with that large class of them who have little learning and religion, and who are thus obliged to use the formulae of modern science as their only vehicle of thought. These men regard humanity as something which started up in Darwin's time. They do not listen when the humanities are mentioned; and if they did they would not understand. When Darwin confessed that poetry had no meaning for him, and nothing significant was left to him in the whole artisitic life of the past, he did not know how many of his brethren his words were destined to describe.[49]

Sir Stephen Spender, in his splendid book on the adaptations of literary culture to the modern world *The Struggle of the Modern* (1963), makes a different and interesting point:

"The literary culture—if one can admit such a term—is a culture because it cultivates the object with the qualities of human personality. There is no such thing as a 'scientific culture' (apart from, perhaps, the group behavior of scientists), because science does not, as such, cultivate objective reality with subjective states of mind which are the result of a long history of civilization. Science simply realizes the true nature of the object, it releases into the stream of life discoveries and inventions which, although they may be chosen for utility or destructive purposes, in themselves incorporate no subjective vision of the individual who discovered or invented them."

Spender should have credited individual scientists with making their discoveries in part because of habits of mind and interests grown from the soil of the broader culture.

---

[49] From *Learning* (1910).

Chapman recognized that this sometimes happens and suggested that the more scientists spent time connecting to the fine arts, the better.

In significant part, this hope has been fulfilled. Indeed, one concern in the world of the 21st Century is the opposite of Chapman's. While scientists are generally open to the full breadth of the humanities in their lives, many people whose lives are based in their religious faith are often hostile to science, not because its practitioners don't appreciate music or the arts, but because the scientific method suggests truths incompatible with those preached to them in church.

Chapman claimed to consider a certain kind of scientist to be essentially a religious practitioner, which, were it more credible, would be cheery news to modern-day creationists and the like who want science considered just another form of faith:

> In these higher regions, in which science is synonymous with the search for truth, science partakes of the nature of religion. It purifies its votaries; it speaks to them in cryptic language, revealing certain exalted realities not unrelated to the realities of music, or of poetry and religion. The men through whom this enthusiasm for pure science passes are surely, each in his degree, transmitters of heroic influence; and, in their own way, they form a kind of priesthood. It must be confessed, too, that this priesthood is peculiarly the product of the nineteenth century.[50]

Chapman reminds us in his essay *The Two Languages*[51] that "Every scientist is a man, and his science surrounded with a nimbus of something which is not

---

[50] From *Learning* (1910).
[51] From *Letters and Religion* (1924).

science and which he cannot shake off." However, Spender's basic point that science, because it operates solely within the realm of facts, cannot directly infuse human culture with meanings and inspirations, is correct. I wonder what Spender or Chapman would think of the changes to human culture resulting from the personal computer, Internet, iPod and web-based everything.

College education focuses its energy and resources on training a generation of students to be good producers in the technical economy, but we are not doing much to enable them to make good judgments about what is right and wrong, what is good and bad. That is what Chapman feared, and what has come to pass.

To counter this we must educate people of all ages to be questioners—no one better epitomized the need to question accepted norms than did Chapman. Questioning is the enemy of dogma; questioning based on an informed individual ethic is a continuous process that refines and improves the life of individuals and the life of society. Thomas Merton noted in a letter to Czeslaw Milosz that

> "there is something wrong with questions that are supposed to be disposed of by answers ... the ideal is to have no more questions. Then when you have no more questions you have peace."[52]

The absence of questions does not mean peace, it means lassitude, stagnation and the submersion of new ideas.

Finally, one thing Chapman found wanting in scientists of the 20th Century, only modestly improved today, was a willingness to emerge from behind the screen of professional language and engage the public:

---

[52] *Striving Towards Being: The Letters of Thomas Merton and Czeslaw Milosz*, Robert Faggen, ed., p. 121 (Farrar Straus Giroux, 1997).

As for science, her lingos have made a psychological chasm between ourselves and the past which is as appalling as the subsidence of Atlantis.[53]

The patriots of the American Revolution—nay, the fathers of modern science, Tyndal, Huxley, Louis Agaziz (sic), Helmholtz—wrote popular books and sought to interest and educate the public by direct contact. Then let the later-coming followers in learning imitate this popular activity of the old leaders: we need a host of battlers for the cause. [54]

[53] From *Our Universities* (1932).
[54] From *Professorial Ethics* (1910).

The Nature of Academic Excellence

If we are to strive to encapsulate in a single concept Chapman's view of college education (and education in general), we could do worse than "serious." To Chapman, education, properly understood and conducted, was a matter of the utmost significance, not only not to be taken lightly, but always to be treated as an opportunity for the more severe kinds of self-improvement. In fact, self-improvement in the most formal sense is another perfectly good way to look at his views. This, after all, is the man who reminded us that "culture is severe."

Chapman has few modern philosophical contemporaries. Certainly such writers on education as Robert Grudin, the late Peter Viereck and the even more late Michael Oakeshott[55] often state views regarding what education is and is not, should and should not be, that would be congenial to Chapman. Andrew Delbanco, in his 2012 book *College*, clearly recognizes that if college is to be meaningful, it has to have content that is excellent, and cannot simply slop along issuing degrees for nonperformance.

Chapman was very practical, from his unique vantage, about what can and cannot (or perhaps should and should not) be done in colleges. He recognized that it is not possible to provide an excellent education for every person, but that society needs to focus on recognizing and

---

[55] Or is Oakeshott less late? A dissertation worth undertaking would study how we describe the dead. For example, I recently heard someone refer to John F. Kennedy as "the late President Kennedy," a full fifty years after his death. Is that how we would describe President Lincoln? Probably not. At what point does someone who is late become merely dead?

supporting excellence when and where it is found, and otherwise providing the basics:

> The higher branches of learning are slow in their effect upon the community. They imply time. If you assist a single first-rate mind to develop fully, that mind will do more for the next age than ten thousand second-rate talents, each of which you should assist a little. That mind can be counted on to educate and inspire its own contemporaries. Thus, in a generation you will have reached everyone. We must be willing to operate down the stream of time. We cannot hope to color all the water of the river as it flows by us; but we can cast something into the stream which will color it down below.[56]

This practicality occasionally collided with his view that all genuine education was defined to include certain things: the classics and humanities as he understood them. Nonetheless, in this age of society's uncompromising commitment to adequacy, constantly defined downward, it is refreshing to encounter commitment to educational excellence in any form, as much for the ideal as the details.

Certainly academic excellence in Chapman's view would include those things that were important to him, set forth in the sections above. Yet clearly his recognition of quality extended across many fields.

At the time Chapman wrote, higher education was still largely in the hands of independent non profit providers, accompanied by major state-based institutions. There were no accrediting associations as we know them today. However, the federal government and the states were starting to become involved in qualitative oversight of

---

[56] From "Art and Art Schools", p. 12-13 in *Memories and Milestones*, reprinted in the *Collected Works of JJC*, vol. 3.

certain programs. In fact, by the early 1900s colleges were already turning their venue-shopping eyes to Washington, as this extract from a federal communication one hundred years ago to President Levi T. Pennington of Oregon's newborn Pacific College (today's George Fox University) shows:

> ... You are entirely correct in assuming that Oregon has the right to determine the qualification of her high school teachers. This she has attempted to do in the law of 1911, and in doing this she has solicited and received the assistance of the United States Bureau of Education. This Bureau, however, does not seek in any way to dictate the standards or the procedure for determining the qualifications of teachers in the state of Oregon.

> ... The practical question of changing through legislation the present method of standardization in Oregon is not one which I ought to discuss beyond saying that special legislation exempting certain institutions from compliance with present standards would be much less desirable than a frank and regular adoption of a lower general standard which would admit certain institutions now excluded even by the liberal interpretation given to the present law.[57]

In other words, we think your college is nowhere near even basic capability, but we'll let the state tell you this (again). This is also an interesting early example of federal interest in state standards.

---

[57] Letter from Kendric le Babraell (a disproportionately rare and spectacular name for an American education bureaucrat of 1912; it might as well have been Abelard) to Pennington, quoted at greater length and with much additional information in Donald McNichols, *Portrait of a Quaker: Levi T. Pennington* (1980).

What does today's society want colleges to do? We are sometimes told by pundits, politicians and thinktankers that colleges should have high academic standards for undergraduates. Unfortunately, society as a whole disagrees. Except in a small number of technical fields and certain high-level sciences, society does not care about "high academic standards" as we in academe would use the phrase.

Outside pressure is for high school and college to be easier (and cheaper), not harder. This was beginning to be true when Chapman wrote and is the norm today. In general, governments are driven by cost, not quality. This philosophy has significant negative consequences when applied to many fields, including education. Debra Humphreys whacks this rusty nail right on its shaky head when she writes that

> ... the completion agenda has morphed into a more-completion-at-less-cost agenda ... whereas society and the economy need "more and *better*," policy leaders are trying to deliver "more and *cheaper*."[58]

As we digest what today's political agendas are, let's keep in view Chapman's reminder that we should "not plant out seventy acres in roses and then swear that they are the finest in the world because there are so many of them."[59]

---

[58] Debra Humphreys, "What's wrong with the completion agenda and what we can do about it." *Liberal Education*, Vol. 98 No. 1, p. 10 (2012).

[59] JJC, "Our Universities," in *New Horizons in American Life*, p. 27 (1932).

Chapman's Principal Essays on Colleges

The following sections include those works which I consider to be Chapman's principal writings on postsecondary education topics. He discusses educational issues, particularly education related to art and religion, in many other writings, but as they are mostly in print in the *Collected Works*, there is no reason to replicate that vast reference here. Here I reprint *Learning* (1910), *Professorial Ethics* (1910), *The Function of a University* (1900, not in the *Collected Works*), *New Dawn in Education* (1926, not in the *Collected Works*) and *Our Universities* (1932).

I have retained Chapman's original typographical errors, of which there are few, and his sometimes brutally long paragraphs, of which there are many. Original pagination is not retained here owing to space limitations, but it is retained in the *Collected Works*.

Chapman's writing on education is much larger than what is presented here and interested readers are referred to the *Collected Works* and to the bibliography that it contains. In addition, Melvin Bernstein's 1964 biography contains a chapter expressly about Chapman's educational ideas.

The Function of a University
(1900)[60]

Youth is not sordid; and the use of a university is that it adds a few years to a man's boyhood, during which his relations to others are not sordid. The problems of life boil down to the question whether one shall be of service to people or shall make use of them; and it makes a great difference whether a man gets his first taste of the issue at the age of 18 or of 22. It makes a great difference, too, whether the intervening years are spent in a counting house, where the very clocks measure nothing but interest, and where the duty to self is preached and practiced at the young man till he feels his nature stiffening into an heroic determination to master this grim and terrible religion of money, or whether those years shall be spent amid surroundings that may awaken the youth to a noble ambition. You may refuse to send your son to a university, you may refuse to have a library in your house, but you cannot greatly disparage the instructive wisdom of mankind which maintains both. There is a utility in them deeper than your cavil. They are perpetual fonts of inspiration for such as know how to use them.

The college buildings, the professors, the games, the societies and the library are a palace of vision. Nothing is spared that can assist vision. The grounds are studded with camerae obscurae showing views of life. But the meaning of these sights is to come afterwards.

If a man is a student while in college he learns to value the accomplishments of valor and intellect; but the cost of

---

[60] This was the lead article in JJC's de facto personal mouthpiece, *The Political Nursery*, Vol. IV No. 5, August, 1900. It appears in the *Collected Works* and was reprinted in *Unbought Spirit*.

them cannot be learned here. The cost remains as unknown as the other side of the moon; language cannot express it. And whether he is a student or not, he lives in an atmosphere of generosity while his bones are setting, and goes out from the place with an integrity which he can, perhaps, never entirely unlearn.

Any one who visits a university feels the influence of a delightful and slightly enervating calm which creeps over him as he crosses the campus. Here are peaceful days and early hours, precision, routine, social happiness. The pictures which the instructors are putting into the slide seem too bright. The instructors themselves appear not to know what tragedies they are handling. The visitor feels he must take the rod from the proctor's hand and give a lecture on the almost imperceptible vestiges of pain still shown on the plate. But the bell rings and it is lunch time. The class in algebra goes on at two.

The lack of vigor in the air of a university comes from the professors. It is impossible for a man to remain at the top of his bent while he is doing anything else but wrestle with new truth; and the temptation of a teacher towards lassitude is overwhelming. He is beyond the reach of new experience, except as he makes it himself in contact with his students and his Faculty; and the man who can make spiritual progress with this outfit is a rare man. The consequence is that most professors go on thinking and teaching the same thing year after year. Give a professor a false thesis in early life, and he will teach it till he dies. He has no way of correcting it.

The rise and progress of new ideas is somewhat as follows: A man makes a discovery; he divulges a theology, or a theory of science or government. If his theory falls into harmony with the current thought of the age, it becomes popular and is taken up on all sides. Years may elapse before a man's theory is adopted by the world at large as being in harmony with accepted notions, and altogether a plausible thing. But when the day of its popularity arrives and no one is any longer afraid of the doctrine, when it is recognized as useful and at any rate as innocuous, then it is adopted by the learned, and professors are established to teach it in the universities, where it smolders and dies away unless it is reinforced from the world. The master minds of the world, whose thoughts have survived change, thus get set before the young of each generation and together with this valuable heritage of thought, mixed in with it, accepted with the same reverence and transmitted with the same zeal, we find all the not-yet-exploded dogmas of contemporary politics, society and trade.

Such were the reflections that passed through my mind as I turned over the journals on a book stall, and noted the flood of essays upon international politics which the professors in our fresh water colleges have recently been pouring upon the world. It is a striking fact that our college professors of economics have been furnishing the arguments for the imperialists. The learning of the land seems to be given over to a crude and bloodthirsty materialism. It is impossible not to be shocked at the heartless rubbish put forth in the name of science, and embellished with absurd technical terms, by men who know as much about war and government as the spinsters and knitters in the sun who weave their thread with bones. The ferocity of these professors puzzled me greatly till I remembered the explanation of it, and then I perceived that these dominies were the mouthpieces of an academic dogma, and were no more to be blamed than their predecessors who had preached infant damnation, no-faith-with-heretics, or any other orthodoxy that was once so canonized by the world as to be regarded as science by a university.

The cause in all such cases must be sought in history. The early formulation of Darwin's discoveries was coeval with an era of great commercial progress. The phrase "struggle for existence," could be understood by everyone, and seemed to justify any form of self-interest. It became popular at once, was labeled science, was widely accepted, and finally it sifted through into the universities where it is taught to-day. It represents a misapprehension of 1850.

The ideal of a university is to encourage thought. But it is a law of nature that thought cannot move forward except through action. Therefore, a university is no sifting place, but only a treasury. It preserves so-much that is really sacred that we can forgive the sanctity it sheds on some ever-changing dross that is shoveled into it and out of it by every passing age. Scientific and prophetic light reaches the university mind thirty years late. Successive dogmas shine down through the elm trees upon leisure and breed pedantry. The pleasant lanes are charged with latent death that makes our pulse beat slower: the lotus is in bloom. We enjoy it for an afternoon and then we cry out "Certainly, this is no place for a grown man." And yet certainly there are no places where grown men are more needed than at the colleges, for the difficulty with these pools of life is to keep open the channels by which the thoughts and feelings of the current world shall run into them.

A thousand new faiths are now forming in the people of the United States; new religions, new forms of spiritual force, and yet such is the constitution of society that they must have passed through the experimental stage before the learned can take note of them. This is due in part to that hiatus in the history of culture which left the mediaeval world at the mercy of the past, and which still stamps all our minds with the instinct that what is of value must be old. It is due in part to the hiatus in our own thought which makes us divide the process of learning from the process of teaching, as if a teacher could have anything more valuable to impart than his own passion to learn the truth. To get professors into your university who want to learn and who have nothing to teach is the way to bring the students as near as possible to the best influences they will meet when they leave your doors. Our western universities have taken a most notable step in filling their chairs of sociology with the younger kind of experimenters. It is true that the torch of the prophet is apt to go out if brought into carbonic acid gas, but on the other hand, the prophet is apt to throw open windows and impart oxygen by which he and all his colleagues may be kept alive. A university ought to be the mere residence of a lot of men who are excited about various aspects of life and history, and who lecture as a means of expressing themselves and of developing their own thought. Their chief corporate bond should be a distrust of each other's society, lest that society come between them and the world. Their great danger is the fixity of their salary and of their entourage, the danger lest this fixity extend itself imperceptibly over their minds. Where such men lived no poppy would bloom, no nerves would grow limp, and the pictures they showed to the young would have in them some tinge of effort and of pain which would imprint them indelibly, and make them hold their own beside the sombre originals which the youth are sure to see at no distant time.

Learning
(1910)[61]

An expert on Greek Art chanced to describe in my hearing one of the engraved gems in the Metropolitan Museum. He spoke of it as 'certainly one of the great gems of the world,' and there was something in his tone that was even more thrilling than his words. He might have been describing the Parthenon or Beethoven's Mass,—such was the passion of reverence that flowed out of him as he spoke. I went to see the gem afterwards. It was badly placed, and for all artistic purposes was invisible. I suppose that, even if I had had a good look at it, I should not have been able to appreciate its full merit. Who could?—save the handful of adepts in the world, the little group of gem-readers, by whom the mighty music of this tiny score could be read at sight. Nevertheless it was a satisfaction to me to have seen the stone. I knew that through its surface there poured the power of the Greek world; that not without Phidias and Aristotle, and not without the Parthenon, could it have come into existence. It carried in its bosom a digest of the visual laws of spiritual force, and was as wonderful and as sacred as any stone could well be. Its value to mankind was not to be measured by my comprehension of it, but was inestimable. As Petrarch felt toward the Greek manuscript of Homer which he owned but could not read, so did I feel toward the gem.

What is Education? What are Art and Religion and all those higher interests in civilization which are always vaguely held up to us as being the most important things in life? These things elude definition. They cannot be put

---

[61] "Learning" appeared as a chapter in *Learning and Other Essays* (1910).

into words except through the interposition of what the Germans call 'a metaphysic.' Before you can introduce them into discourse, you must step aside for a moment and create a theory of the universe; and by the time you have done this, you have perhaps befogged yourself and exhausted your readers. Let us be content with a more modest ambition. It is possible to take a general view of the externals of these subjects without losing reverence for their realities. It is possible to consider the forms under which art and religion appear,—the algebra and notation by which they have expressed themselves in the past,—and to draw some general conclusion as to the nature of the subject, without becoming entangled in the subject itself.

We may deal with the influence of the gem without striving exactly to translate its meaning into speech. We all concede its importance. We know, for instance, that the admiration of my friend the expert was no accident. He found in the design and workmanship of the intaglio the same ideas which he had been at work on all his life. Greek culture long ago had become a part of this man's brain, and its hieroglyphs expressed what to him was religion. So of all monuments, languages, and arts which descend to us out of the past. The peoples are dead, but the documents remain; and these documents themselves are part of a living and intimate tradition which also descends to us out of the past,—a tradition so familiar and native to the brain that we forget its origin. We almost believe that our feeling for art is original with us. We are tempted to think there is some personal and logical reason at the back of all grammar, whether it be the grammar of speech or the grammar of architecture,—so strong is the appeal to our taste made by traditional usage. Yet the great reason of the power of art is the historic reason. 'In this manner have these things been expressed: in similar manner must they continue to be said.' So speaks our artistic instinct.

Good usage has its sanction, like religion or government. We transmit the usage without pausing to think why we do so. We instinctively correct a child, without pausing to reflect that the fathers of the race are speaking through us. When the child says, 'Give me a apple,' we correct him—"You must say, 'An apple.'" What the child really means, in fact, is an apple.

All teaching is merely a way of acquainting the learner with the body of existing tradition. If the child is ever to have anything to say of his own, he has need of every bit of this expressive medium to help him do it. The reason is, that, so far as expressiveness goes, only one language exists. Every experiment and usage of the past is a part of this language. A phrase or an idea rises in the Hebrew, and filters through the Greek or Latin and French down to our own time. The practitioners who scribble and dream in words from their childhood up,—into whose habit of thought language is kneaded through a thousand reveries,—these are the men who receive, reshape, and transmit it. Language is their portion, they are the priests of language.

The same thing holds true of the other vehicles of idea, of painting, architecture, religion, etc., but since we have been speaking of language, let us continue to speak of language. Expressiveness follows literacy. The poets have been tremendous readers always. Petrarch, Dante, Chaucer, Shakespeare, Milton, Goethe, Byron, Keats— those of them who possessed not much of the foreign languages had a passion for translations.

It is amazing how little of a foreign language you need if you have a passion for the thing written in it. We think of Shakespeare as of a lightly-lettered person; but he was ransacking books all day to find plots and language for his plays. He reeks with mythology, he swims in classical metaphor: and, if he knew the Latin poets only in translation, he knew them with that famished intensity of interest which can draw the meaning through the walls of a bad text. Deprive Shakespeare of his sources, and he could not have been Shakespeare.

Good poetry is the echoing of shadowy tongues, the recovery of forgotten talent, the garment put up with perfumes. There is a passage in the Tempest which illustrates the free-masonary of artistic craft, and how the weak sometimes hand the torch to the mighty. Prospero's apostrophe to the spirits is, surely, as Shakespearian as anything in Shakespeare and as beautiful as anything in imaginative poetry.

"Ye elves of hills, brooks, standing lakes and groves;
 And ye, that in the sands with printless foot
 Do chase the ebbing Neptune, and do fly him,
 When he comes back; you demi-puppets, that
 By moonshine do the sour ringlets make,
 Whereof the ewe not bites; and you whose pastime
 Is to make midnight mushrooms that rejoice
 To hear the solemn curfew; by whose aid
 (Weak masters though ye be) I have bedimmed
 The noontide sun, called forth the mutinous winds,
 And 'twixt the green sea and the azur'd vault
 Set roaring war: to the dread rattling thunder
 Have I given fire, and rifted Jove's stout oak
 With his own bolt: the strong-bas'd promontory
 Have I made shake; and by the spurs pluck'd up
 The pine and cedar: graves at my command
 Have waked their sleepers; oped and let them forth
 By my so potent art."

Shakespeare borrowed this speech from Medea's speech in Ovid, which he knew in the translation of Arthur Golding; and really Shakespeare seems almost to have held the book in his hand while penning Prospero's speech. The following is from Golding's translation, published in 1567:

"Ye Ayres and windes; ye Elves of Hilles and Brooks, of
Woods alone,
Of standing Lakes and of the Night approach ye every
chone.
Through helpe of whom (the crooked banks much
wondering at the thing)
I have compelled streams to run clean backward to their
spring.
By charmes I make the calm seas rough, and make the
rough Seas plaine.
And cover all the Skie with Clouds and chase them thence
again.

By charmes I raise and lay the windes, and burst the
Viper's jaw.
And from the bowels of the Earth both stones and trees
doe draw.
Whole woods and Forestes I remove: I make the
Mountains shake,
And even the Earth it selfe to grone and fearfully to quake.
I call up dead men from their graves: and thee O lightsome
Moone
I darken oft, though beaten brasse abate thy perill soone.
Our Sorcerie dims the Morning faire, and darkes the
Sun at Noone. The flaming breath of fierie Bulles ye
quenched for my sake.

50

And caused their unwieldie neck the bended yokes to take.
Among the earthbred brothers you a mortell war did set
And brought a sleepe the dragon fell whose eyes were
never shut."

There is, and is to be, no end of this reappearance of
old metapor [sic], old trade secret, old usage of art. No
sooner has a masterpiece appeared, that summarizes all
knowledge, than men get up eagerly the next morning with
chisel and brush, and try again. Nothing done satisfies. It is
all in the making that the inspiration lies; and this endeavor
renews itself with the ages, and grows by devouring its
own offspring.

The technique of any art is the whole body of
experimental knowledge through which the art speaks. The
glazes of pottery become forgotten and have to be hit
upon over again. The knack of Venetian glass, the
principle of effect in tiles, in lettering, in the sonnet, in the
fugue, in the tower,—all the prestidigitation of art that is
too subtle to be named or thought of, must yet be acquired
and kept up by practice, held to by constant experiment.

Good artistic expression is thus not only a thing done:
it is a way of life, a habit of breathing, a mode of
unconsciousness, a world of being which records itself as it
unrolls. We call this world Art for want of a better name;
but the thing that we value is the life within, not the shell
of the creature. This shell is what is left behind in the
passage of time, to puzzle our after-study and make us
wonder how it was made, how such complex delicacy and
power ever came to co-exist. I have often wondered over
the Merchant of Venice as one wonders over a full-blown
transparent poppy that sheds light and blushes like a cloud.
Neither the poppy nor the play were exactly hewn out:
they grew, they expanded and bloomed by a sort of inward

power,—unconscious, transcendent. The fine arts blossom from the old stock,—from the poppy-seed of the world.

I am here thinking of the whole body of the arts, the vehicles through which the spirit of man has been expressed. I am thinking also of the sciences,—whose refractory, belligerent worshipers are even less satisfied with any past expression than the artists are, for their mission is to destroy and to rearrange. They would leave nothing alive but themselves. Nevertheless, science has always been obliged to make use of written language in recording her ideas. The sciences are as much a part of recorded language as are the arts. No matter how revolutionary scientific thought may be, it must resort to metaphysics when it begins to formulate its ultimate meanings. Now when you approach metaphysics, the Greek and the Hebrew have been there before you- are very near to matters which you never intended to approach. You are back at the beginning of all things, human thought does not advance, it only recurs. Every tone and semi-tone in the scale is a keynote; and every point in the Universe is the centre of the Universe; and every man is the centre and focus of the cosmos, and through him passes the whole of all force, as it exists and has existed from eternity; hence the significance which may at any moment radiate out of anything.

The different arts and devices that time hands to us are like our organs. They are the veins and arteries of humanity. You cannot rearrange them or begin anew. Your verse-forms and your architecture are chosen for you, like your complexion and your temperament. The thing you desire to express is in them already. Your labors do no more than enable you to find your own soul in them. If you will begin any piece of artistic work in an empirical spirit and slave over it until it suits you, you will find yourself obliged to solve all the problems which the artists have been engaged on since the dawn of history. Be as independent as you like, you will find that you have been anticipated at every point: you are a slave to precedent, because precedent has done what you are trying to do, and, ah, how much better! In the first place, the limitations, the horrible limitations of artistic possibility, will begin to present themselves; few things can be done: they have all been tried: they have all been worked to death: they have all been developed by immortal genius and thereafter avoided by lesser minds,—left to await more immortal genius. The field of endeavor narrows itself in proportion to the greatness of the intellect that is at work. In ages of great art everyone knows what the problem is and how much is at stake. Masaccio died at the age of twenty-seven, after having painted half a dozen pictures which influenced all subsequent art, because they showed to Raphael the best solution of certain technical questions. The Greeks of the best period were so very knowing that everything appeared to them ugly except the few attitudes, the few arrangements, which were capable of being carried to perfection.

Anyone who has something to say is thus found to be in one sense a slave, but a rich slave who has inherited the whole earth. If you can only obey the laws of your slavery, you become an emperor: you are only a slave in so far as you do not understand how to use your wealth. If you have but the gift of submission, you conquer. Many tongues, many hands, many minds, a traditional state of feeling, traditional symbols,—the whole passed through the eyes and soul of a single man,— such is art, such is human expression in all its million-sided variety.

II

I have thrown together these remarks in an elliptical and haphazard way, hoping to show what sort of thing education is, and as a prologue to a few reflections upon the educational conditions in the United States. It is easy to think of reasons why the standards of general education should be low in America. Almost every influence which is hostile to the development of deep thought and clear feeling has been at the maximum of destructive power in the United States. We are a new society, made of a Babel of conflicting European elements, engaged in exploiting the wealth of a new continent, under conditions of climate which involve a nervous reorganization to Europeans who come to live with us. Our history has been a history of quiet colonial beginnings, followed by a national life which, from its inception, has been one of social unrest. And all this has happened during the great epoch of the expansion of commerce, the thought-destroying epoch of the world.

Let us take a rapid glance at our own past. In the beginning we were settlers. Now the settlement of any new continent plays havoc with the arts and crafts. Let us imagine that among the Mayflower pilgrims there had been a few expert wood-carvers, a violin player or two, and a master architect. These men, upon landing in the colony, must have been at a loss for employment. They would have to turn into backwoodsmen. Their accomplishments would in time have been forgotten. Within a generation after the landing of the pilgrims there must have followed a decline in the fine arts, in scholarship, and in certain kinds of social refinement. This decline was, to some extent, counteracted in our colonial era by the existence of wealth in the Colonies and by the constant intercourse with Europe, from which the newest models were imported by every vessel. Nevertheless, it is hard for a colony to make up for its initial loss; and we have recently seen the United States government making efforts on a large scale to give to the American farmer those practices of intensive cultivation of the soil which he lost by becoming a backwoodsman and has never since had time to recover for himself.

The American Revolution was our second set-back in education. So hostile to culture is war that the artisans of France have never been able to attain to the standards of workmanship which prevailed under the old monarchy. Our national culture started with the handicap of a seven years' war, and was always a little behindhand. During the nineteenth century the American citizen has been buffeting the waves of new development. His daily life has been an experiment. His moral, social, political interests and duties have been indeterminate; nothing has been settled for him by society. Is a man to have an opinion? Then he must make it himself. This demands a more serious labor than if he were obliged to manufacture his own shoes and candlesticks. No such draught upon individual intellect is made in an old country. You cannot get a European to understand this distressing over-taxing of the intelligence in America. Nothing like it has occurred before, because in old countries opinion is part of caste and condition: opinion is the shadow of interest and of social status.

But in America the individual is not protected against society at large by the bulwark of his class. He stands by himself. It is a noble idea that a man should stand by himself, and the conditions which force a man to do so have occasionally created magnificent types of heroic manhood in America. Lincoln, Garrison, Emerson, and many lesser athletes are the fruits of these very conditions which isolate the individual in America and force him to think for himself. Yet their effect upon general cultivation has been injurious. It seems as if character were always within the reach of every human soul; but men must have become homogeneous before they can produce art. We have thus reviewed a few of the causes of our American loss of culture. Behind all these causes, however, was the true and overmastering cause, namely, that sudden creation of wealth for which the nineteenth century is noted, the rise all over the world of new and uneducated classes. We came into being as a part of that world movement which has perceptibly retarded culture, even in Europe. How, then, could we in America hope to resist it ? Whether this movement is the result of democratic ideas, or of mechanical inventions, or of scientific discovery, no one can say. The elements that go to make up the movement cannot be unraveled. We only know that the world has changed: the old order has vanished with all its charm, with all its experience, with all its refinement. In its place we have a crude world, indifferent to everything except physical well-being. In the place of the fine arts and the crafts we have business and science. Business is, of course, devoted to the increase of physical well-being; but what is Science? Now, in one sense, science is anything that the scientific men of the moment happen to be studying. In one decade, science means the discussion of spontaneous generation, in the next of germs, or of electrodes. Whatever the scientific world takes up as a study becomes "science." It is impossible to deny the truth of this rather self-destructive definition. In a more serious sense, however, science is the whole body of organized knowledge; and a distinction is sometimes made between "pure" science and "applied" science; the first being concerned solely with the ascertainment of truth, the second, with practical matters.

In these higher regions, in which science is synonymous with the search for truth, science partakes of the nature of religion. It purifies its votaries; it speaks to them in cryptic language, revealing certain exalted realities not unrelated to the realities of music, or of poetry and religion. The men through whom this enthusiasm for pure science passes are surely, each in his degree, transmitters of heroic influence; and, in their own way, they form a kind of priesthood. It must be confessed, too, that this priesthood is peculiarly the product of the nineteenth century.

The Brotherhood of Science is a new order, a new Dispensation. It would seem to me impossible to divide one's feeling toward science according to the divisions "pure" and "applied"; because many men in whom the tide of true enthusiasm runs the strongest deal in applied science, as, for instance, surgeons, bacteriologists, etc. Nor ought we to forget those great men of science who have an attitude of sympathy toward all human excellence, and a reverence for things which cannot be approached through science. Such men resemble those saints who have also, incidentally, been kings and popes. Their personal magnitude obliterates our interest in their position in the hierarchy. We think of them as men, not as popes, kings or scientists. In the end we must admit that there are as many kinds of science as there are of men engaged in scientific pursuits. The word science legitimately means an immense variety of things, loosely connected together, some of them deserving of strong reprobation. I shall use the term with such accuracy as I am able to command, and leave it to the candid reader to make allowance for whatever injustice this course may entail.

To begin with, we must find fault with the Brotherhood of Science on much the same ground that we fought the old religions, grounds of tyranny and narrowness, and presumption. In the next place, it is evident that, in so far as science is not hallowed by the spirit of religion, it is a mere extension of business. It is the essence of world-business, race-business, cosmic-business. It saves time, saves lives, and dominates the air and the sea; but all these things may be accomplished, for ought we know, in the course of the extinction of the better nature of mankind. Science is not directly interested in expression of spiritual truth; her notation cannot include anything so fluctuating, so indeterminate, as the language of feeling. Science neither sings nor jokes; neither prays nor rejoices; neither loves nor hates. This is not her fault; but her limitation. Her fault is that, as a rule, she respects only her own language and puts trust only in what is in her own shop window.

I deprecate the contempt which science expresses for anything that does not happen to be called science. Imperial and haughty science proclaims its occupancy of the whole province of human thought; yet, as a matter of fact, science deals in a language of its own, in a set of formulae and conceptions which cannot cover the most important interests of humanity. It does not understand the value of the fine arts and is always at loggerheads with philosophy. Is it not clear that science, in order to make good her claim to universality, must adopt a conception of her own function that shall leave to the fine arts and to religion their languages? She cannot hope to compete with these languages, nor to translate or expound them. She must accept them. At present she tramples upon them.

There are, then, in the modern world these two influences which are hostile to education,— the influence of business and the influence of uninspired science. In Europe these influences are qualified by the vigor of the old learning. In America they dominate remorselessly, and make the path of education doubly hard. Consider how they meet us in ordinary social life. We have all heard men bemoan the time they have spent over Latin and Greek on the ground that these studies did not fit them for business,—as if a thing must be worthless if it can be neither eaten nor drunk. It is hard to explain the value of education to men who have forgotten the meaning of education: its symbols convey nothing to them.

The situation is very similar in dealing with scientific men,—at least with that large class of them who have little learning and religion, and who are thus obliged to use the formulae of modern science as their only vehicle of thought. These men regard humanity as something which started up in Darwin's time. They do not listen when the humanities are mentioned; and if they did they would not understand. When Darwin confessed that poetry had no meaning for him, and nothing significant was left to him in the whole artisitic life of the past, he did not know how many of his brethren his words were destined to describe.

We can forgive the business man for the loss of his birthright: he knows no better. But we have it against a scientist if he under-values education. Surely, the Latin classics are as valuable a deposit as the crustacean fossils, or the implements of the Stone Age. When science shall have assumed her true relation to the field of human culture we shall all be happier. Today science knows that the silkworm must be fed on the leaves of the mulberry tree but does not know that the soul of man must be fed on the Bible and the Greek classics. Science knows that a queen bee can be produced by care and feeding, but does not as yet know that every man who has had a little Greek and Latin in his youth belongs to a different species from the ignorant man. No matter how little it may have been, it reclassifies him. There is more kinship between that man and a great scholar than there is between the same man and some one who has had no classics at all: he breathes from a different part of his anatomy. Drop the classics from education ? Ask rather, Why not drop education? For the classics are education. We cannot draw a line and say, 'Here we start.' The facts are the other way. We started long ago, and our very life depends upon keeping alive all that we have thought and felt during our history. If the continuity is taken from us, we shall relapse.

When we discover that these two tremendous interests—business and commerical [sic] science have arisen in the modern world and are muffling the voice of man, we tremble for the future. If these giants shall continue their subjugation of the gods, the whole race, we fear, way [sic] relapse into dumbness. By good fortune, however, there are other powers at work. The race is emotionally too rich and too much attached to the past to allow its faculties to be lost through disuse. New and spontaneous crops will soon be growing upon the mould of our own stubbly, thistle-bearing epoch.

In the meantime we in America must do the best we can. It is no secret that our standards of education are below those of Europe. Our art, our historical knowledge, our music and general conversation, show a stiffness and lack of exuberance—a lack of vitality and of unconscious force—the faults of beginners in all walks of life. During the last twenty-five years much improvement has been made in those branches of cultivation which depend directly upon wealth. Since the Civil War there seems to have been a decline in the higher literature, accompanied by an advance in the plastic arts. And more recently still there has been a literary reawakening, perhaps not of the most important kind, yet signifying a new era. If I may employ an obvious simile, I would liken America to a just-grown man of good impulses who has early advantages. He feels that cultivation belongs to him; and yet he cannot catch it nor hold it. He feels the impulse of expression, and yet he can neither read nor write. He feels that he is fitted for general society, and yet he has no current ideas or conversation. And, of course—I say it with regret, but it is a part of the situation—of course he is heady and proud of himself.

What do we all desire for this ingenuous youth on whom the postponed expectation of the world, as Emerson called it, has waited so long? We desire only to furnish him with true advantages. Let us take a simultaneous survey of the two extremities of the youth's education, namely, of nursery training and of the higher education. The two are more intimately dependent upon each other than is generally suspected. With regard to the nursery, early advantages are the key to education. The focus of all cultivation is the fireside. Learning is a stove plant that lives in the cottage and thrives during the long winter in domestic warmth. Unless it be borne into children in their earliest years, there is little hope for it. The whole future of civilization depends upon what is read to children before they can read to themselves. The world is powerless to reconvey itself through any mind that it has not lived in from the beginning,— so hard is the language of symbols, whether in music, or in poetry, or in painting. The art must expand with the heart, as a hot rod of glass is touched by the gold-leaf, and is afterwards blown into dusty stars and rainbows of mantling irradiation. If the glass expand before it has been touched by the metal, there is no means of ever getting the metal into it.

The Mind On Edge

The age of machinery has peopled this continent with promoters and millionaires, and the work of a thousand years has been done in a century. The thing has, however, been accomplished at some cost. An ignorant man makes a fortune and demands the higher education for his children. But it is too late: he should have given it to them when he was in his shirt sleeves. All that they are able to receive now is something very different from education. In receiving it they drag down the old standards. School and college are filled with illiterates. The whole land must patiently wait till Learning has warmed back to life her chilled and starved descendants. Perhaps the child or grandchild of the fortune-builder will teach the children on his knee what he himself learned too late in life to stead him much.

Hunger and thirst for learning is a passion that comes, as it were, out of the ground; now in an age of wealth, now in an age of poverty. Young men are born whom nothing will satisfy except the arts and the sciences. They seek out some scholar at a university and aim at him from boyhood. They persuade their parents to send them to college. They are bored and fatigued by everything that life offers except this thing. Now, society does not create this hunger. All that society can do is to provide nourishment of the right kind, good instruction, true learning, the best scholarship which history has left behind. I believe that to-day there is a spirit of learning abroad in America—here and there, in the young—the old insatiable passion. I feel as if men were arising—most of them still handicapped by the lack of early training—to whom life has no meaning except as a search for truth. This exalted famine of the young scholar is the hope of the world. It is religion and art and science in the chrysalis. The thing which society must beware of doing is of interposing between the young learner and his natural food some mechanical product or patent food of its own. Good culture means the whole of culture in its original sources; bad culture is any substitute for this.

Let us now examine the higher departments of education, the university, the graduate school, the museum,—the learned world in America. There is one function of learned men which is the same in every age, namely, the production of text-books. Learned men shed text-books as the oak sheds acorns, and by their fruits ye shall know them. Open almost any primary text-book or school book in America, and you will, on almost every page of it, find inelegancies of usage, roughnesses, inaccuracies, and occasional errors of grammar. The book has been written by an incompetent hand. Now, what has the writer lacked? Is it grammar ? Is it acquaintance with English literature, with good models, with the Bible, with history? It is all these things, and more than all. No school-room teaching can make a man write good English. No school teaching ever made an educated man, or a man who could write a good primary text-book. It requires a home of early culture, supplemented by the whole curriculum of scholarship and of university training, Nothing else but this great engine will produce that little book.

The same conditions prevail in music. If you employ the nearest excellent young lady music teacher to teach your boys to play the piano, she will bring into the house certain child's music written by American composers, in which the rules of harmony are violated and of which the sentiment is vulgar. The books have been written by incompetent people. There is a demand for such books and they are produced. They are the best the times afford: let us be glad that they exist at all and that they are no worse. But note this: it will require the whole musical impulse of the age, from the oratorio society and the musical college down to the street organ, to correct the grammar of that child's music book. Ten or twenty years from now a like book will perhaps be brought into your home, filled with better harmony and with truer musical feeling; and the change will have been wrought through the influence of Sebastian Bach, of Beethoven,— of the masters of music. It is the same with all things. The higher culture must hang over the cradle, over the professional school, over the community. If you read the lives of the painters of Italy or of the musicians of Germany, you will find that, no matter where a child of genius was born, there was always an educated man to be found in the nearest village—a priest or a schoolmaster—who gave the child the rudiments himself, and became the means of sending him to the university. Without this indigent scholar, where would have been the great master ?

It is familiarity with greatness that we need— an early and first-hand acquaintance with the thinkers of the world, whether their mode of thought was music or marble or canvas or language. Their meaning is not easy to come at, but in so far as it reaches us it will transform us. A strange thing has occurred in America. I am not sure that it has ever occurred before. The teachers wish to make learning easy. They desire to prepare and peptonize and sweeten the food. Their little books are soft biscuit for weak teeth, easy reading on great subjects; but these books are filled with a pervading error: they contain a subtle perversion of education.

Learning is not easy, but hard; culture is severe. The steps to Parnassus are steep and terribly arduous. This truth is, often forgotten among us; and yet there are fields of work in which it is not forgotten, and in such fields art springs up. Let us remember the accomplishments of our country. The art in which we now most excel is architecture. America has in it many beautiful buildings and some learned architects. And how has this come about? Through severe and conscientious study of the monuments of art, through humble, old-fashioned training. The architects have had first-rate text-books, generally written by Europeans, the non-peptonized, gritty, serious language of masters in the craft. Our painters have done something of the same sort. They have gone to Europe, and are conversant with what is being done in Europe. If they are developing their art here, they do it not ignorantly, but with experience, with consciousness of the past.

I do not recommend subserviency to Europe, but subserviency to intellect. Recourse to Europe we must have: our scholars must absorb Europe without themselves becoming absorbed. It is a curious thing that the American who comes in contact with the old world exhibits two opposite faults: he is often too much impressed and loses stamina, or he is too little impressed and remains a barbarian. Contact with the past and hard work are the cure for both tendencies. Europe is merely an incidental factor in the problem of our education, and this is very well shown in our conduct of our law schools. The Socratic method of instruction in law schools was first introduced at Harvard, and since then it has spread to many parts of the world. This is undoubtedly one of our best achievements in scholarship; and Europe had, so far as I know, no hand in it. The method consists in the viva voce discussion of leading cases, text-books being used merely as an auxiliary: the student thus attacks the sources themselves. Here we have American scholarship at its best, and it is precisely the same thing as the European article: it is simply scholarship.

If we can exhibit this spirit in one branch of learning, why not in all? The Promethean fire is one single element. A spark of this fire is all that is needed to kindle this flame. The glance of a child of genius at an Etruscan vase leaves the child a new being. That is why museums exist: not only for the million who get something from them, but for the one young person of intelligence to whom they mean everything.

Our American universities exhibit very vividly all the signs of retardation in culture, which are traceable in other parts of our social life. A university is always a stronghold of the past, and is therefore one of the last places to be captured by new influence. Commerce has been our ruler for many years; and yet it is only quite recently that the philosophy of commerce can be seen in our colleges. The business man is not a monster; but he is a person who desires to advance his own interests. This is his occupation and, as it were, his religion. The advancement of material interests constitutes civilization to him. He unconsciously infuses the ideas and methods of business into anything that he touches. It has thus come about in America that our universities are beginning to be run as business colleges. They advertise, they compete with each other, they pretend to give good value to their customers. They desire to increase their trade, they offer social advantages and business openings to their patrons. In some cases they boldly conduct intelligence offices, and guarantee that no hard work done by the student shall be done in vain: a record of work is kept during the student's college life, and the college undertakes to furnish him at any time thereafter with references and a character which shall help him in the struggle for life.

This miscarriage of education has been developed and is being conducted by some of our greatest educators, through a perfectly unconscious adaptation of their own souls to the spirit of the age. The underlying philosophy of these men might be stated as follows: "There is nothing in life nobler than for a man to improve his condition and the condition of his children. Learning is a means to this end." Such is the current American conception of education. How far we have departed from the idea of education as a search for truth, or as the vehicle of spiritual expression, may be seen herein. The change of creeds has come about innocently, and the consequences involved in it are, as yet, perceived by hardly anyone. The scepticism inherent in the new creed is concealed by its benevolence. You wish to help the American youth. This unfortunate, benighted, ignorant boy, who has from his cradle heard of nothing but business success as the one goal of all human effort, turns to you for instruction. He comes to you in a trusting spirit, with reverence in his heart, and you answer his hope in this wise: 'Business and social success are the best things that life affords. Come to us, my dear fellow, and we will help you toward them.' Your son asks you for bread and you give him a stone, for fish and you give him a serpent. It would have been better for that boy if he had never come to your college, for in that case he might have retained a belief that somewhere in the world there existed ideas, art, enthusiasm, unselfishness, inspiring activity. In so far as our universities have been turning into business agencies, they have naturally lost their imaginative importance. Our professors seem to be of little more consequence in the community that the department managers of other large shops. If learning is a useful commodity which is to be distributed for the personal advantage of the recipients, it is a thing to be paid for rather than to be worshiped. To be sure, the whole of past history cannot be swept away in a day, and we have not wholly discarded a certain conventional and rhetorical reverence for learning. A dash and varnish of education are thought to be desirable, — the wash that is growing every year more thin.

Now, the truth is that the higher education does not advance a man's personal interests except under special circumstances. What it gives a man is the power of expression; but the ability to express himself has kept many a man poor. Let no one imagine that society is likely to reward him for self-expression in any walk of life. He is much more likely to be punished for it. The question of a man's success in life depends upon society at large. The more highly an age is educated, the more highly it rewards education in the individual. In an age of indifference to learning, the educated man is at a disadvantage. Thus the thesis that education advances self-interest—that thesis upon which many of our colleges are now being conducted—is substantially false. The little scraps and snatches of true education which a man now gets at college often embarrass his career. Our people are finding this out year by year, and as they do so, they naturally throw the true conception of the higher education overboard. If education is to break down as a commercial asset, what excuse have they for retaining it at all ? They will force the colleges to live up to the advertisements and to furnish the kind of education that pays its way. It is clear that if the colleges persist in the utilitarian view, the higher learning will disappear. It has been disappearing very rapidly, and can be restored only through the birth of a new spirit and of a new philosophic attitude in our university life.

There are ages when the scholar receives recognition during his lifetime and when the paths which lead to his lecture-room are filled with men drawn there by his fame.

This situation arises in any epoch when human intellect surges up and asserts itself against tyranny and ignorance. In the past the tyrannies have been political tyrannies, and these have become well understood through the struggles of intellect in the past; but the present commercial tyranny is a new thing and as yet little understood. It lies like a heavy fog of intellectual depression over the whole kingdom of Mammon, and is fed by the smoke from a million factories. The artist works in it, the thinker thinks in it. Even the saint is born in it. The rain of ashes from the nineteenth-century Vesuvius of business seems to be burying all our landscape.

And yet this is not true. We shall emerge: even we who are in America and suffer most. The important points to be watched are our university class-rooms. If our colleges will but allow something unselfish, something that is true for its own sake, something that is part of the history of the human heart and intellect to live in their class-rooms, the boys will find their way to it The museum holds the precious urn, to preserve it. The university, in like manner, stands to house the alphabets of civilization——the historic instruments and agencies of intellect. They are all akin to each other as the very name and function of the place imply. The presidents and professors who sit beside the fountains of knowledge bear different labels and teach subjects that are called by various names. But the thing which carries the label is no more than the shell. The life you cannot label; and it is to foster this life that universities exist. Enthusiasm comes out of the world and goes into the university. Toward this point flow the currents of new talent that bubble up in society: here is the meeting-place of mind. All that a university does is to give the poppy-seed to the soil, the oil to the lamp, the gold to the rod of glass before it cools. A university brings the spirit in touch with its own language, that language through which it has spoken in former days and through which alone it shall speak again.

Professorial Ethics
(1910)[62]

When I was at a university as an undergraduate—I will not say how many years ago—I received one morning a visit from a friend who was an upper classman; for, as I remember it, I was a freshman at the time. My friend brought a petition, and wished to interest me in the case of a tutor or assistant professor, a great favorite with the college boys, who was about to be summarily dismissed. There were, to be sure, vague charges against him of incompetence and insubordination; but of the basis of these charges his partisans knew little. They only felt that one of the bright spots in undergraduate life surrounded this same tutor; they liked him and they valued his teaching. I remember no more about this episode, nor do I even remember whether I signed the petition or not. The only thing I very clearly recall is the outcome: the tutor was dismissed.

Twice or thrice again during my undergraduate life, did the same thing happen—a flurry among the students, a remonstrance much too late, against a deed of apparent injustice, a cry in the night, and then silence. Now, had I known more about the world, I should have understood that these nocturnal disturbances were signs of the times, that what we had heard in all these cases was the operation of the guillotine which exists in every American institution of learning, and runs fast or slow according to the progress of the times. The thing that a little astonished the undergraduate at the time was that in almost every case of summary decapitation the victim was an educated

---

[62] "Professorial Ethics" appeared as a chapter in *Learning and Other Essays* (1910).

gentleman. And this was not because no other kind of man could be found in the faculty. It seemed as if some whimsical fatality hung over the professorial career of any ingenuous gentleman who was by nature a scholar of the charming, old-fashioned kind.

Youth grieves not long over mysterious injustice, and it never occurred to me till many years afterward that there was any logical connection between one and another of all these judicial murders which used to claim a passing tear from the undergraduate at Harvard. It is only since giving some thought to recent educational conditions in America, that I have understood what was then happening, and why it was that a scholar could hardly live in an American University.

In America, society has been reorganized since 1870; the old universities have been totally changed and many new ones founded. The money to do this has come from the business world. The men chosen to do the work have been chosen by the business world. Of a truth, it must needs be that offenses come; but woe be unto him through whom the offense cometh. As the Boss has been the tool of the business man in politics, so the College president has been his agent in education. The colleges during this epoch have each had a "policy" and a directorate. They have been manned and commissioned for a certain kind of service, as you might man a fishing-smack to catch herring. There has been so much necessary business—the business of expanding and planning, of adapting and remodeling—that there has been no time for education. Some big deal has always been pending in each college —some consolidation of departments, some annexation of a new world—something so momentous as to make private opinion a nuisance. In this regard the colleges have resembled everything else in America. The colleges have simply not been different from the rest of American life. Let a man express an opinion at a party caucus, or at a railroad directors' meeting, or at a college faculty meeting, and he will find that he is speaking against a predetermined force. What shall we do with such a fellow? Well, if he is old and distinguished, you may suffer him to have his say, and then override him. But if he is young, energetic, and likely to give more trouble, you must eject him with as little fuss as the circumstances will permit.

The educated man has been the grain of sand in the college machine. He has had a horizon of what "ought to be," and he could not help putting in a word and an idea in the wrong place; and so he was thrown out of education in America exactly as he was thrown out of politics in America. I am here speaking about the great general trend of influences since 1870, influences which have been checked in recent years, checked in politics, checked in education, but which it is necessary to understand if we would understand present conditions in education. The men who, during this era, have been chosen to become college presidents have, as a rule, begun life with the ambition of scholars; but their talents for affairs have been developed at the expense of their taste for learning, and they have become hard men. As toward their faculties they have been autocrats, because the age has demanded autocracy here; as toward the millionaire they have been sycophants, because the age has demanded sycophancy here. Meanwhile these same college presidents represent learning to the imagination of the millionaire and to the imagination of the great public. The ignorant millionaire must trust somebody; and whom he trusts he rules. Now if we go one step further in the reasoning, and discover that the millionaire himself has a somewhat exaggerated reverence for the opinions of the great public, we shall see that this whole matter is a coil of influence emanating from the great public, and winding up—and generally winding up very tight—about the necks of our college faculties and professional scholars. The millionaire and the college president are simply middle men, who transmit the pressure from the average citizen to the learned classes. What the average citizen desires to have done in education gets itself accomplished, though the process should involve the extinction of the race of educated gentlemen. The problem before us in America is the unwinding of this "knot intrinsicate" into which our education has become tied, the unwinding of this boa-constrictor of ignorant public opinion which has been strangling and, to some extent, is still strangling our scholars.

I have no categorical solution of the problem, nor do I, to tell the truth, put an absolute faith in any analysis of social forces, even of my own. If I point out one of the strands in the knot as the best strand to begin work on, it is with the consciousness that there are other effectual ways of working, other ways of feeling about the matter that are more profound.

The natural custodians of education in any age are the learned men of the land, including the professors and schoolmasters. Now these men have, at the present time, in America no conception of their responsibility. They are docile under the rule of the promoting college president, and they have a theory of their own function which debars them from militant activity. The average professor in an American college will look on at an act of injustice done to a brother professor by their college president, with the same unconcern as the rabbit who is not attacked watches the ferret pursue his brother up and down through the warren, to predestinate and horrible death. We know, of course, that it would cost the non-attacked rabbit his place to express sympathy for the martyr; and the non-attacked is poor, and has offspring, and hopes of advancement. The non-attacked rabbit would, of course, become a suspect, and a marked man the moment he lifted up his voice in defense of rabbit-rights. Such personal sacrifice seems to be the price paid in this world for doing good of any kind. I am not, however, here raising the question of general ethics; I refer to the philosophical belief, to the special theory of professorial ethics, which forbids a professor to protect his colleague. I invite controversy on this subject; for I should like to know what the professors of the country have to say on it. It seems to me that there exists a special prohibitory code, which prevents the college professor from using his reason and his pen as actively as he ought in protecting himself, in pushing his interests, and in enlightening the community about our educational abuses. The professor in America seems to think that self-respect requires silence and discretion on his part. He is too great to descend into the arena. He thinks that by nursing this gigantic reverence for the idea of professordom, such reverence will, somehow, be extended all over society, till the professor becomes a creature of power, of public notoriety, of independent reputation as he is in Germany. In the meantime, the professor is trampled upon, his interests are ignored, he is overworked and underpaid, he is of small social consequence, he is kept at menial employments, and the leisure to do good work is denied him. A change is certainly needed in all of these aspects of the American professor's life. My own opinion is that this change can only come about through the enlightenment of the great public. The public must be appealed to by the professor himself in all ways and upon all occasions. The professor must teach the nation to respect learning and to understand the function and the rights of the learned classes. He must do this through a willingness to speak and to fight for himself. In Germany there is a great public of highly educated, nay of deeply and variously learned people, whose very existence secures pay, protection, and reverence for the scholar. The same is true in France, England, and Italy.

It is the public that protects the professor in Europe. The public alone can protect the professor in America. The proof of this is that any individual learned man in America who becomes known to the public through his books or his discoveries, or his activity in any field of learning or research, is comparatively safe from the guillotine. His position has at least some security, his word some authority. This man has educated the public that trusts him, and he can now protect his more defenseless brethren, if he will. I have often wondered, when listening to the sickening tale of some brutality done by a practical college president to a young instructor, how it had been possible for the eminent men upon the faculty to sit through the operation without a protest. A word from any one of them would have stopped the sacrifice, and protected learning from the oppressor. But no, these eminent men harbored ethical conceptions which kept them from interfering with the practical running of the college. Merciful heavens! who is to run a college if not learned men? Our colleges have been handled by men whose ideals were as remote from scholarship as the ideals of the New York theatrical managers are remote from poetry. In the meanwhile, the scholars have been dumb and reticent.

At the back of all these phenomena we have, as I have said, the general atmospheric ignorance of the great public in America. We are so used to this public, so immersed in it, so much a part of it ourselves, that we are hardly able to gain any conception of what that atmospheric ignorance is like. I will give an illustration which would perhaps never have occurred to my mind except through the accident of actual experience. If you desire a clue to the American in the matter of the higher education, you may find one in becoming a school trustee in any country district where the children taught are the children of farmers. The contract with any country school-teacher provides that he shall teach for so many weeks, upon such and such conditions. Now let us suppose a teacher of genius to obtain the post. He not only teaches admirably, but he institutes school gardens for the children; he takes long walks with the boys, and gives them the rudiments of geology. He is in himself an uplifting moral influence, and introduces the children into a whole new world of idea and of feeling. The parents are pleased. I will not say that they are grateful; but they are not ungrateful. It is true that they secretly believe all this botany and moral influence to be rubbish; but they tolerate it. Now, let us suppose that before the year is out the teacher falls sick, and loses two weeks of school time through absence. You will find that the trustees insist upon his making up this lost time; the contract calls for it. This seems like a mean and petty exaction for these parents to impose upon a saint who has blessed their children, unto the third and fourth generation, by his presence among them. But let us not judge hastily. This strange exaction does not result so much from the meanness of the parents, as from their intellectual limitations. To these parents the hours passed in school are schooling; the rest does not count. The rest may be pleasant and valuable, but it is not education.

In the same way, the professional and business classes in America do not see any point in paying salaries to professors who are to make researches, or write books, or think beautiful thoughts. The influence which an eminent man sheds about him by his very existence, the change in tone that comes over a rude person through his once seeing the face of a scholar, the illumination of a young character through contact with its own ideals—such things are beyond the ken of the average American citizen to-day. To him, they are fables, to him they are foolishness. The parent of our college lad is a farmer compared to the parent of the European lad.

The American parent regards himself as an enlightened being—yet he has not, in these matters, an inkling of what enlightenment is. Now, the intelligence of that parent must be reached; and the learned classes must do the work of reaching it. The Fathers of the Christian church made war with book and speech on Paganism. The leaders of the Reformation went out among the people and made converts. The patriots of the American Revolution—nay, the fathers of modern science, Tyndal, Huxley, Louis Agaziz, Helmholtz—wrote popular books and sought to interest and educate the public by direct contact. Then let the later-coming followers in learning imitate this popular activity of the old leaders: we need a host of battlers for the cause.

For whom do these universities exist, after all? Is it not for the people at large? Are not the people the ultimate beneficiaries? Then why should the people not be immediately instructed in such manner as will lead to their supporting true universities ? It is hard to say why our professors are so timid. Perhaps too great a specialization in their own education has left them helpless, as all-around fighters. But the deeper reason seems to be a moral one; they think such activity is beneath them. It is not beneath them. Whatever be a man's calling, it is not beneath him to make a fight for the truth. As for a professor's belonging to a mystic guild, no man's spiritual force is either increased or diminished by the name he calls his profession. Learning is their cause, and every honest means to promote learning should be within their duty. Nor does duty alone make this call for publicity. Ambition joins in it; the legitimate personal ambition of making one's mind and character felt in the world. This blow once struck means honor, and security of tenure in office, it means public power.

In fine, the scholars should take the public into their confidence and dominate the business men on our college boards. This will be found more easy than at first appears, because the money element, the millionaire element, is very sensitive to public feeling, and once the millionaire succumbs, the college president will succumb also. The step beyond this would consist in the scholars' taking charge of the college themselves, merely making use of certain business men on their boards for purposes of financial administration.

The New Dawn in Education
(1926)[63]

The symposium on Education which THE FORUM published last month is a good sign of the times. It is a great thing when the scholars of a country rouse themselves and speak with authority. It was the sign of a new epoch when, in 1837, Emerson delivered his famous Phi Beta Kappa address, which was in fact followed by a revival of intellect and of literacy in America. The tone of censure which vibrated in Emerson offended many persons, for our politicians had all but convinced everyone that we Americans were the advanced guard of civilization, — the glory of the human race, —when, behold, a Jeremiah arose, rent his garments, and cried, "Perhaps the time has come when the sluggard intellect of this continent will look from under its iron eyelids and fill the postponed expectation of the world with something better than the exertion of mechanical skill."

When a scholar steps forward in defense of his own calling he is at a great advantage, for he not only knows his own subject but knows how to talk; and if he happens to be fired with anguish or with indignation, so much the better.

The materialism of our own age has grown to be so noisy, gigantic, and overpowering that one looks back on the Massachusetts of Emerson's day, with its mills and streams, as a kind of Arcadia. To-day the cranes, steam-shovels, and skeleton towers; the unceasing sound of the drills; the yawning caverns of excavation, make suburban life ugly and turn city life into a nightmare. Our mind and

[63] In *The Forum* Vol. LXXV 75 No. 4, April 1926 p. 606-609.

spirit seem to partake of the pandemonium that reigns without and we murmur, "Can the soul of a people survive this epoch?" The question hovers in each thoughtful heart, certainly something has happened to us that never happened before in history.

Such rapid changes as we have undergone during the last fifty years, — changes in every form of education and avocation, in the habits and aspirations of our people, and in the make-up of the population itself, — never took place before in any nation except through external conquest, — through the dissoluton of one civilization by the imposition of another. And yet we have not been conquered, — at least from without, — and all that we see is but the blossoming of certain seeds that were always with us and which grew and spread with such vigor as apparently to crowd out all other forms of vegetation.

The most palpable change which began to come over us about seventy years ago was the gradual but steady fading out of the influence of the thoughtful classes in the country. Our men of mind became scattered and shadowy personalities. The authority of intellect survived as towards the specialists, but there was ever less of that vaguer reverence for character and intellect which is in its nature a religious emotion. Piety and the respect for past history and for human experience were all but lost with us. We lived ever more and more in the present.

In Europe the learned classes constitute a great phalanx of enthusiasts who spend their energies in keeping alive all that is great, true, and permanent in past history. They act as powerful stabilizers of the general consciousness of nations and serve to anchor them in the intellectualinheritances of the world. But we in America had become so engrossed in our daily pursuits that we had almost forgotten that there was such a thing as world-wisdom, when, at the beginning of the twentieth century, a new impulse ran through the land.

It was Dean West of Princeton who first recalled the country to its senses by his indefatigable activity in the cause of true scholarship, and by his many papers and addresses in which our situation was summed up with adequacy, with absolute courage, and with bonhomie. Whatever may be the future history of the Graduate School at Princeton, its foundation marked a turning-point in American civilization. It was a monument large enough to be seen. It was articulate, specific, enduring, and it proclaimed the need of a return to liberal studies. "And liberal they truly are," said West, "for they are the studies which supremely enfranchise, universalize, and elevate human nature the world over."

It is worth noting that this resurgence of humanism appeared first in a university, the place where in theory it ought to have arisen, — in the place where (to quote Browning)

. . . man's thought
Rarer, intenser,
Self-gathered for an outbreak, as it ought,
Chafes in the censer.

While we must agree that a university is a furnace whence the flames of new thought should issue, or a mountain that ought to break into eruption now and then, we know also that the general state of cultivation in any country has a great deal to do with such explosions. Universities are also thermometers, and they not only record the boiling point but the freezing point of learning. Many people in America think that, in spite of Dean West's efforts, a well-defined zero is to be discerned in our own seats of the higher education. In order to find the cause of this we must look abroad into the lives, homes, occupations, and ambitions of our people at large, and find out where it is that the fires have gone out.

Our scholars have begun to examine these questions. The simultaneous appearance of two books, one about university life, and the other on school problems, has recently given us a panoramic view of what is taking place in the hearts of many American educators who are finding their way back to those ideals of character and conduct, of religion and literacy which are the most precious possessions of mankind. One of the books is in the form of a Report to President Hopkins of Dartmouth College by Mr. Leon B. Richardson, and is called *A Study of the Liberal College,* It takes up each subject in the shape in which the question meets the college professor; and, moreover, it is written by a man of the world, and its pages are full of wit, irony, and practical wisdom. The second book is in the form of a round robin. Seven men, the headmasters of our well-known private schools, have contributed papers, each on a separate aspect of school life. The volume is entitled *The Modern Boy.*

Both these books reflect the same spirit: On the questions of the Home, of Athletics, Scholarship, "Leadership", "Activities" of the "Average Man", and the "Influence of Money;" they speak the same thoughts, smoulder with the same indignation, and break forth into the same images. Each of them represents a revolt against custom, and the breakdown of the shibboleths of Democracy as applied to Education. They deal with the subject, not by the light of sociological dogmas, but by the light of the laws of Nature. The notion that an educator's first duty is toward the child of talent has sprung up quite suddenly all over our country. The suspicion has dawned on us that we have been spending too much time over the lower two-thirds of the class, and neglecting the bright scholars because they seemed to take care of themselves, — to give no trouble and perhaps to need no attention. We never before had stopped to reflect that these talented boys were our future editors, statesmen, writers, and divines, and that the quickest way to raise the general average was to do our best by them and let them loose on the community; that it was *they* who would raise the general tone and temper of our intellectual life and set a pace for the others.

The fact is that people are influenced not so much by their elders as by their contemporaries, and if you will but train the exceptional boy to the height of his capacity his influence will do for his own generation something that you yourself can never do. Our recent recognition of the claim made by talent is of most hopeful and most profound significance. It is a recognition of what might be called the first natural law of education; to him that hath shall be given. So rapidly does life move on that the present widespread re-awakening in the United States to the meaning of this natural law will probably show in our general literacy within half a generation.

It is by following one or two great ideas, and by gradually adapting and remodeling our school systems and our university systems to them, that real progress will be made, Both systems are to-day so full of makeshifts, malpractises, and absurdities that it is error to try to amend them by any great frontal attack. They must be eased up here and there according to the illumination of the persons in charge.

We are all familiar with the extravagances and, as it were, the crazes that rage in our university life, the craze of the administrators for building and for expansion in every form, and the craze of the students for athletics, fraternities, and distractions in every form; for the making of acquaintances that will be of use in a future business career, and for the taking of courses that will help to get them jobs on graduation. The students bring these ideals with them from their firesides,—or rather from their steam-heated apartments in tall buildings. They come in shoals, the rich ones from an environment of sport, pleasure, and social excitement which they hope to continue in college and return to on leaving college; and the poor ones with a determination to make college an ante-chamber to a life of business success with as much sport, pleasure, and social excitement in it as college can teach them. The early training of the richer students is closely related to the famished visions of the poorer students, and both classes are about as eager for cultivation as a red Indian would be who, having been bred in the woods and sent to a seminary, longs for the forest, the tomahawk, and the chase.

Such are the main outlines of our university life: the eyes of the college president are on vast schemes of expansion, and the eyes of the student are on pleasure. Let us now look beyond the boundaries of the university and note the larger national conditions which our colleges reflect, Whether we examine our political or our business methods, our press, our theatre, or our social life, we find the same giddiness and superficiality,—a sort of super-normal love of the excitements of the moment. The proofs of our strangely depleted mental condition and of its cause lie on all sides, and every road leads to them. Today we in America are passing through in access, a tornado, a frenzy of prosperity. Can we survive it? Shall we be rescued by some timely difficulties that create a wholesome moral pressure; or shall we lose all the strong, manly qualities that blessed our origins, and go under, as so many nations have done, through the indolence of pride, luxury, and comfort? The danger that faces the Republic arises, as we all know, from the destructive power of wealth. Almost all the degradations that we see in the United States can be traced to the influence of prosperity.

Is it not clear that the administrators of our colleges merely exhibit one variety of money-madness and their students another? How can one hope to reform or civilize either of those elements, the administrators who are afflicted with a mania for grandeur or the boys in their charge who feel Business in their blood, — Business, as it were, the Call of the Wild?

It is easy to see that the love of money is at the root of both diseases, just as this love is the explanation of almost everything that is happening about us in America today. But what are you going to do about it? Can you banish the love of pleasure from the American breast or put a barrier between the great public and college football? Can you examine the smile of each applicant for admission to college and take the silver spoons from the mouths of the sons of profiteers as they pass in? Would it help for a millionaire to raise the salary of every professor in some small college to $50,000 a year; or to import a dozen Oxford dons and plant them about a campus? Such devices would do no good. Mr. Richardson in his book on the Liberal College sees all the distortions and follies of our college life with a calm eye, the expense and fanatic fury of the athletics, the childishness and heartburn of the fraternities, the reflection in college life of that contempt for superior intelligence or special talent which qualifies our Democracy, and a hundred other points of which every professional educator feels the prick. But Mr. Richardson does not propose to abolish athletics or to invade the fraternities with hostile legislation, He has many a trenchant page on the evils of college life but his remedy is always the same:

"To raise in the great body of the students interest and ideals which will make them, not scholars in the technical sense but men in whom the intellectual appeal strikes a responsive note and insures an understanding and sympathetic response,—that is what is meant by scholarship." We must apply ourselves to making strong and effective and primary the intellectual purpose of the college. "Before the undergraduate can be convinced, or the public can be convinced, those who guide the institution must themselves be convinced of the principle." This is somewhat like saying, Seek first the kingdom of heaven and all those things will be added unto you; and that is why I like it. It avoids laying down any dogma, yet suggests that the cure is within reach.

The composite book, written by headmasters of our best known private schools, is equally frank and more militant. We are apt to conceive of educators as dogmatic persons, perhaps even as supercilious and pompous men. But these men are beating their breasts. They proclaim their dilemmas frankly and ask for aid in their search for the remedies. The scorching flames of the iniquities that rage in the country at large have been felt by the authors. Certain deadly tendencies of the times are seen more keenly by the schoolmaster than by the university professor, perhaps because a schoolmaster deals with childhood, and it is upon the child that the devastation is most visibly working.

Dr. Stearns of Phillips Andover Academy, after giving some truly terrifying statistics about the juvenile crime in the country at large, says: "Again we must face facts. Wealth and social position may add a superficial refinement to human frailties, but neither wealth nor position can change the innate nature of such weaknesses nor alter their ultimate effect on character; and the heads of schools that deal with these boys and girls from the homes of the well-to-do, are as deeply disturbed and as keenly alarmed over the breakdown of home standards and influences as are their colleagues who guide the destinies of our high schools:

"The utter and unpatriotic lawlessness of so many of the older generation, blessed with wealth and social standing, is one of the strange anomalies of the times. . . . Lawless parents cannot hope for better than lawless children. Homes in which parental authority has been banished, discipline and restraint abolished, idealism quenched, and spiritual values discarded, can never produce high-minded and effective citizens."

This is cutting near the bone, and I leave the reader to reorganize his opinions on our fashionable schools, as I was obliged to reorganise my own, after reading the volume; for I had been inclined to regard such schools as places controlled by the ideals of their clientele.

Dr. Peabody of Groton says, "There is no thought of giving an able boy as advanced instruction as he is capable of receiving. ... In the English schools a pupil is carried on as rapidly as he can profitably travel. Promotion may be gained at any time of the year. He may reach the upper form at an early age, much below his time for university life, and there in the upper class . . . become a highly trained scholar. Such an ideal is possible to us. We have a supply of boys who are capable . . . and many of our masters are able to give this higher instruction."

Dr. Thayer of St Mark's School, Southborough, whose paper is a masterly brief for the independence of the private school, says, "The future trends of the private school, if it is to be wholesome and progressive, must begin with a declaration of independence of college examinations." "The sole contention is that the school period is the time for making the scholar and not for preparing him to be made in college." "Democracy can only continue to exist if the individual, superior in mind, character or personal power, has the opportunity to rise above his fellows. By the same token, a private school has no right to exist within a democracy if its aim be the education of the average gained by the neglect or suppression of the superior."

Such thoughts as these on education represent a crossing of a Rubicon by the American Mind.

Our Universities
(1932)[64]

In man's intercourse with man there are two Languages — the Language of the Intellect and the Language of the Emotions; or, if you will, Science and the Fine Arts. The language of the emotions is divided into various dialects — Poetry, Painting, Music, etc. We call them the Humanities.

The symbols of science are accurate and convey the same meaning to every scientist. On the other hand, the symbols of the humanities are fluid and convey a different meaning to each individual.

The era which we are passing through is an age of science. Open any scientific journal. Our land is filled with such a blaze of genius in the fields of technical and applied science as reminds one of art during the Italian Renaissance or music in Germany in the eighteenth century. Every branch of science is organized and concatenated between the abstract and the concrete, the theorist and the inventor, the manufacturer and the consumer. The great machine whizzes and dazzles. The carpet of opportunity is unrolled before early scientific talent as it was before the infant Mozart. Science is today the popular language that is drawing the world together, and many people think that it is taking up the mission of the old humanities: the two are often mingled together in the public mind. But the two Empires of Science and the

[64] "Our Universities" was originally a lecture presented at Columbia University in 1931. It was later published as one of two essays in *New Horizons in American Life* (1932) and is reproduced here courtesy Columbia University Press. It is also included in the *Collected Works of John Jay Chapman* (1970).

Humanities are in truth governed by two different kinds of force. The first is automatic and is recorded and manipulated by instruments and mathematical calculations. The second is personal and is recorded in aesthetic and philosophic symbols and traditions. Science cannot say a kind word, make a joke or turn a tune. Science has neither heart, lungs, body, taste nor feeling. It detects what the eye cannot see and records what the ear cannot hear. It transmits man's various voices, but has no voice of its own. It is more silent than the sphinx.

In Commander Byrd's expedition to the Antarctic there was assembled such a complete outfit of the apparatus of science as had never before been brought together into so small a compass. The latest devices for observing and recording natural phenomena—astronomy, meteorology, natural history, geology, geography—in all the symbols which science has devised, were the important part of the venture. Yet Commander Byrd had not forgotten those fields of human endeavor which he had left behind in the North. His taking a Boy Scout to the South Pole was a gesture of reverence made by science to a language which it cannot speak. In that case science bowed its head quite naturally, sincerely, lovingly, to that sound-heartedness in the American people which is our best quality. This living sympathy is the same passion that should flicker between the schoolmaster and his boys, between the professor and his students. It springs from a consciousness of the unity of human nature, and a desire to transmit to future generations all the pieties of the race.

Our present age was ushered in by Benjamin Franklin in the eighteenth century. It may well be described as the age predicted by Jules Verne. It advanced with such fury as to transform the externals of man's life upon the globe and almost to persuade him that they are the whole of it, or at

least the most important part. For three or four
generations we rushed to the window to see a comet or a
fire engine, throwing aside our chisels and pens, our
brushes and our lutes. On returning to pick them up, we
find ourselves a bit rusty and out of practice. Our senses
have become blunted by the cruelty of mechanical
reproductions, the starkness of photography, the clatter of
the phonograph, the crudity of diagrams. As for science,
her lingos have made a psychological chasm between
ourselves and the past which is as appalling as the
subsidence of Atlantis. The devil-machines of science have
reproduced for our benefit the pictures of the past—
falsified in monochrome and polychrome—the voices of
the past shorn of their overtones, the past dehumanized of
its envelopes, ticketed and ticked off.

All such devices are infinitely useful in a thousand
ways —and so is strychnine, which they somewhat
resemble in their effects—but we must not confound these
devices with the fine arts and the handicrafts, with poetry,
music, dancing or good conversation, which are
transmissible only from mind to mind in the studio, in the
market place, the drawing-room, the workshop. We must
not be beguiled and led astray by these miracles of
mechanical reproduction, or they will kill in us the creative
inspirations of art.

The boundaries between these two major provinces,
science and the humanities, are very distinct; and yet they
have become confused in the public mind, and sometimes
even in the minds of important men of science. The chief
difference between science and art is this, that the
statements and conclusions of science can be verified.
They all depend upon measurements and calculations on
which all the professional scientists of the world agree. But
as to music and painting and poetry, the meanings and

messages they bring differ with each listener or observer or reader. A second difference is that science comes to stay because it is a utility. It is a constant and cumulative possession. The ages of art pass like clouds: they cannot be arrested. Whistler put the idea plainly in the best thing he ever said: "There is no such thing as Art: there are only artists." There is really no way of verifying the power and significance of a painting or of a poem or of an essay. And yet there is great public curiosity about the meaning of our emotions, especially of our religious feelings.

A curious thing has happened in regard to this matter. The popular enthusiasm for scientific advance has, of late years, led our people to call on distinguished scientists for news of the next world, for theories of morality, advice about sex and the fine arts, etc., and some of them have responded quite frankly that they know no more about such things than we do. The greatest scientists of the ages have in their own lives illustrated the fact that it is the search for truth that ennobles men. The field to which a man devotes himself is of lesser consequence.

There is yet another difference between science and the emotional arts. Both the theories and the verifications of science are arrived at by a tension of the intellectual faculties. With the fine arts it is different. In order to sound a note that carries, the artist and his instrument must be possessed and enveloped in a vortex of feeling which obliterates the very means that create the blast and leaves only a message of emotion. So far as any verification is possible, it comes through receptivity, self-abandonment and repose. Chopin's highest praise, when listening to a pupil's performance was, *rien ne me choque.*[65]

---

[65] "Nothing shocks me." JJC may have seen this statement discussed in his colleague William James's "What is an Emotion", an article published in *Mind* in 1884.

It is a good thing for a devotee either of science or of the fine arts to rest his mind with a study of the other—for the poet to read a scientific journal as a diversion, and for the mathematician to go to a concert. In an age like our own, which is engrossed in close thinking and in practical results, in the exclusion of all emotional factors from the mind, men become unfitted for painting and writing and poetry, for composing and playing music, for singing and acting—arts in which the technical difficulties are surrounded by a nimbus and cloud of emotion which directs and controls them. Science demands clear thinking and nothing else. The shutting out of emotional disturbance from his thought went so far with Darwin that he could no longer enjoy music or Shakespeare's plays; and something of the kind has been happening to the children of this Age of Science. Perhaps the very men who might have been our poets have become our geologists, mathematicians and astronomers.

It would, indeed, be a normal reaction in any era that has been mad for science if it should be followed by a revival of the fine arts. There are signs that such a reaction is in progress all over the world today. The smoldering embers of archaeology have always been the source from which the fine arts were fired. When Peisistratus edited Homer, in the sixth century B.C., he was preserving a monument. The professional reciters had kept the Iliad and the Odyssey alive for a thousand years by an appeal to the passion for archaeology in the breast of the Greek peoples. It was this same instinct of conservation that governed the rise of sculpture and painting in Italy and, later, vitalized the literatures of Europe at the time of the Revival of Learning. Indeed archaeology—in this wider sense—and art are so commingled that one cannot say which is which. To take a small domestic illustration,

Henry Ford could not tell you why he collects old furniture. He has been touched by an influence that is in the air—the breath of a new era that has been wafted across Europe ever since the discoveries at Troy, Mycenae and Tiryns. This was the antitoxin for a mechanical age. The general reception of it showed the need of it. Schliemann was the rising star of a new era which began, as always, long before the passing age had reached its climax. These discoveries of Schliemann aroused an enthusiasm, a craving, which science had been powerless to satisfy. The objects found at Mycenae were thought to be the arms and adornments of the best-known mythical figures in European history. Had these objects been commonplace they would have excited only passing notice; but they were beautiful, precious, marvelous works of art. They were immediately reproduced and expounded in hundreds of popular books. Ever since the discoveries of Schliemann a new flame has been burning in all the universities and museums of the world. The later finds have come like rockets at midnight. Crete, Egypt, Sumer, have become lands of promise and the Ultima Thule of romance. The daily literature of exploration has become so great that a man must devote his whole time to it to keep track of it. In Walter Scott's day an antiquary was a solitary old fellow who poked about for the traces of a Roman wall. Today he is the best scholar in your classical department, who sets out for Mesopotamia with the equipment of an engineer, the learning of a historian and the feelings of a poet.

The old humanities are the vehicles by which man has recorded his inner experiences—his religion, his love, his hopes and fears, his social feelings and domestic life—his soul's history. All the old arts and crafts spring from deep roots in human nature and are entwined in the history of civilization. They are interwoven and interlocked with one another. The meanings of the older records are deciphered or guessed at by the meanings found in the later records. The whole series is a congeries of hieroglyphics, from the caves of Altamira to the tabloid found in an afternoon paper. Any acquaintance with any part of the record passes into the current social life of the world and affects the race indefinitely.

The survival of Greek literature civilized the Romans, and the Revival of Learning transformed the mind of modern Europe. You will say that it is a strange thing that man should advance by looking backward, yet it seems to be a fact that literature and the fine arts have always been the outcome of man's endeavor to reconstruct an imaginary past. We sit, as it were, with our backs to the driver and can only deal with what we see, or think we see, in the past. Any acquaintance with the past fertilizes our minds. This assumption has always been taken as the basis of all education. It is the corner stone on which every school and university in the world has been founded. The notion that we belong to the future seems to sterilize a man—as may be seen in those recent attempts in painting, poetry and music in which the author consciously endeavors to separate himself from the past. The future is a cold mystery, the past is warm with life.

I have hazarded my remarks thus far as a prelude to the subject of education. "The School and College Curriculum" is a deadly phrase, and does not convey the idea which alone makes education of value—namely, inspiration. For the essence of education is to inspire, and this is a matter of personal influence, and about it there always hangs a mystery. Between mother and child, teacher and schoolboy, professor and student, great thinker and lesser thinker on any subject, there flows an unnamable power which conveys the import of the matter in hand, whether it be a song from Mother Goose or a problem in astronomy. The invention of printing somewhat clouded this subject and made us tend to accept a book for a man. In the early days of the Revival of Learning it was the very person of the great teacher toward whom the students flocked; and this is still the case with the great masters of medicine, physics, embryology, chemistry, etc. The same attraction of personality is seen today in the case of popular poets, novelists and dramatists. The larger public feels a desire to see the person of any author who has stimulated them. Thus our lecture halls are crowded with commuters who listen to foreign authors and get inspiration from the contact. Your bright boy of six is taken to see the great actor in Hamlet. He ought, if you can manage it, to be taken to see every great man who passes through town. If our eyes could be opened to the nature of things, we should see no books or textbooks, but only the human influences behind them. Let us take the case of the mother who is talking to her baby, or that of a primary schoolmistress who is teaching the alphabet to a small child, or, if you prefer, that of the latest editor of Oedipus, who is reading the play in a seminar with a group of postgraduate students. The child in the first two cases and the students in the third are getting more from the teacher than from the book.

I have drawn my illustrations from the earliest steps in education and from the latest ones. If you seek for examples of good teaching in America in any stage between the two, the nursery and the seminar, you will find it hard to discover one. And if you glance out of the window at any passing child or youth, with his twenty pounds of books in a satchel, you will see the disease that is ravaging our young people.

The American mind pictures education as a succession of long lanes with hurdles in them which the scholar must leap over. The hurdles are books. The teacher is as much harnessed by regulations as the scholars. The whole system is designed to shackle personal influence. Every point in this system—which ought to distribute spiritual energy—is furnished with a nonconductor.

Meanwhile there is probably not a high school in the land that does not contain one or two boys who are fitted by nature and disposition for a life of scholarship. A youth of this sort ought to walk home with the master after class, and on passing to the university, should carry a line of introduction to the head of its Latin department. You smile. It is nevertheless worth while to consider things that seem to be impossible, for they sometimes give the key to the future. That a boy should walk home with his teacher involves the infiltration of a new spirit into our education and the general acceptance of a very simple truth which to the American mind seems incomprehensible—namely, that education is not baggage but power.

The best teaching that I have ever experienced was at the Harvard Law School in the late eighties. Each class meeting was an inquest. Professor Ames, after saying good morning to the large roomful of youths who sat as silent and intent as if they were about to listen to a Beethoven quartet, would state the point at issue and, in answer to a raised hand, would say: "Perhaps Mr. Johnson will tell us his view." After that, the discussion would take such a form as general interest and his own guidance by quiet suggestion gave to it. The men left the room stimulated, eager, enthusiastic. They dispersed slowly: the discussion was continued in scattered groups as they went to luncheon.

When my boys were at Harvard, I used occasionally to attend their English classes and listen in. I remember a Freshman class in English Composition in which the instructor was using a textbook. He was teaching the boys that "prose is divided into narrative, argumentative and"—something else. I examined the book. It was a monstrous and horrible piece of dogmatic nonsense. I waited after class and, seeing that the instructor was an intelligent and benevolent young man, I asked him why he did not throw away the book and teach the boys what he knew. "I can't," he said; "it's prescribed."

There you have a sample of that system of schedules and textbooks which crystallizes the blood in both teacher and scholar in our American schools and colleges. It is due to a reliance on the punching of tickets at the gateways of entrances and exits. I could lie awake at night thinking of the fate of all those American men and women who take up teaching as a profession and spend their lives working the tickers invented by persons who should have been employed in drawing up railroad timetables. Even our college authorities dare not rely on their own judgment in appointing a second assistant professor. They need the moral support of some document which establishes the man's competency: they require the backing of a Ph.D. Almost any kind of Ph.D. will suffice; and the applicant must take a year and write a thesis which will, very likely, leave him less inspiring as a teacher than he was before he wrote it.

Our marking system—the grading of everything by percentages—has been borrowed from business life and fantastically developed into a kind of amateur psychology. Your American believes that you can express anything whatever by figures. The dons at Oxford who received the Rhodes scholars were somewhat puzzled by the decimal fractions as to merit with which the American educators had documented the applicants, especially by the points for "Leadership," so-called, which appeared in some of the certificates. The dons waited in order to find out by experience what these points for Leadership might mean; and one of them is said to have written to the American shippers, "Please do not send us any more 'Leaders.'"

I picked up an anecdote at Oxford that shows the difference between the British idea of education and our own. A don is in charge of a Rhodes scholar and says to him: "Go to such an alcove, read the books on William Pitt and bring me a paper on him." The boy goes and after a time reappears with his essay. The don says on examining it: "But you have brought me only facts. I want ideas." The boy goes again and returns with another paper which the don reads. He exclaims again: "Why, you have simply copied out other people's opinions. I am not interested in them. I want your own." "Oh" cries the boy, "if I should do that in America, they'd say 'Hot air!'"

A similar case occurred with my son Victor at the age of ten, when he was at a private preparatory school of the first order. He was a dreamy child, and when asked in a geography examination "What are the exports of Italy?" he sank into a contemplation and finally hazarded "Pomegranates." "Nothing of the sort!" exclaimed the teacher indignantly; "the book says not a word of pomegranates." Now Victor's mother was half Italian. He had heard of pomegranates and perhaps had seen one.

Our American system is the same from baby classes up to Rhodes scholarships. The absurd decimals used in our marking system give a boy a false view of the whole subject of education. Moreover, they hold down and shackle the schoolmaster and press the life out of him. His life is at best a treadmill. He has to repeat the same function every day. He explains the same problem, translates the same passage, year after year, till he hardly knows who is at the other side of the desk. The experience of teaching somewhat cages a man. He becomes a subspecies of humanity. Your village schoolmaster has always been an isolated personage; your college don tends to become a prig; your professor, a mandarin. In Germany, where the humanities are regarded as a branch of science, the learned write exclusively for each other, making use of a hieratic language which protects them from the curiosity of the vulgar. Members of the teaching class everywhere are apt to carry their profession in their eyes, and even when they do not, society is afraid of them. When I was in college, visiting foreigners used to wonder why the Harvard professors were never asked to dine out in Boston; for there were three or four of them who would have added brilliancy to a dinner party in London, Paris or Berlin.

I cannot pass on from this point without taking off my hat to England, where the doors of the great houses are thrown open to every man of distinction in any field of human endeavor—a custom which perhaps England caught from France in the latter part of the eighteenth century. The tendency to eliminate scholars from polite life is strong in the United States—if one may call a tendency strong which is grounded on two kinds of weakness, the pride of the scholar and the timidity of his hostess.

The humanities are not learning itself, but the fruits of learning. They are a means of enlarging our powers of enjoyment, of sympathy and of communication with others. They are fields of thought that lie between man and man, while universities are in theory the roof that stretches over man's whole intellectual kingdom. Universities draw their life from the people at large and become mirrors, symbols and microcosms of the community. In every age universities have reflected the social, political and religious preoccupations of the day. Every one of them has pictured an epoch, and an epoch is a natural product. No man makes an epoch: every man is a consequence, a creature of his age. And so also every university is a consequence of its age.

In glancing at our American universities today one sees that they embody the traditions and reflect the ideals of our contemporary life much as the universities of 1300 embodied the ideals and traditions of the Middle Ages. Our social conditions, our literary and philosophic thought, our amusements, hygiene, private convictions, personal ambitions, are strikingly exhibited in our university life. It goes without saying that these institutions should today be run as branches of executive business, because this is the only kind of management that our present age understands.

It is in vain that you argue with one of our university managers that the aim of a university is to connect the mind of the student with the thought of the ages. He wishes to prepare the student for the life of the day. He regards himself as the Messiah of education. This is just the attitude of the rich men and religious persons who gave endowments to colleges in the Middle Ages. They desired so to mold the imaginations of the young that the young should see life as they themselves saw it.

Now it has happened that the last quarter of the nineteenth century was marked by the spectacular rise of big business in America, and the change was naturally reflected in our universities. The startling transformation of our old, somnolent halls or shanties of learning into gigantic factories of business men, which took place between 1870 and 1900, is a credit to the public spirit of our leading citizens. But it came about so suddenly and involved so much building, planning and operating that our benefactors and their subordinates, the college authorities, forgot that any kind of talent except business talent was required in the conduct of a university. The transformation was governed by the thought of the whole American people. Science was adopted as their dogma, and the manuals of science as their prayer books. Science took the place which Dogma once held in the medieval universities; and Business, the daughter of Science, was given the niche in the rotunda once filled by Theology. The faithful were helped to find jobs on graduation; for a degree amounted to a certificate of orthodoxy. Our colleges thus became intelligence offices.

The sight of the new buildings blinds a man. They remind you of new meerschaum pipes, and one suspects that it will require a few generations of students to color them. They suggest the present so violently that one needs smoked glasses to avoid being made dizzy by them. Some months ago I visited one of the new quadrangles at Harvard, and I was particularly struck with the library. It was large and luxurious, with extravagantly comfortable armchairs, electricity in all forms, rugs, tables, atlases—and two thousand books, all new, blazing from the walls with gilt titles; and beneath them a couple of golfers reading the newspapers. This library, for the use of young scholars, was done in the taste of a millionaire's yacht club.

This transformation of our older universities came so suddenly and involved such tremendous financial commitments that the managers are obliged to serve the passing age and provide such surroundings as the benefactors will pay for and as the general public will support. Our colleges have become, as it were, the racing-stables of competing millionaires, and the whole movement of university-building has become a kind of national sport. But one cannot say that this is an unmixed evil. There is an ethical element in sport. The competing merchants of Athens paid enormous sums for the staging of the tragedies of Aeschylus and Sophocles. Our colleges are today constantly reviving Greek plays, and their graduates present them with stadia and open-air theaters. Tomorrow these same benefactors may subscribe to raise the salary of the Greek professor. The present age is so sensitively organized that a sincere revival of scholarship in any small college would be felt and reflected everywhere. All depends on what shall go forward in the breasts of the American people outside of the universities.

At any rate it can never be said that we have not thoroughly tried out the experiment of a mass production of the humanities. It does not work: we must try other methods. We wish to encourage the race and breed of scholars. What shall we do? If it were a question of fine roses, everyone knows that you must place a few of them under favorable conditions and cultivate them. You do not plant out seventy acres in roses and then swear that they are the finest in the world because there are so many of them. The building at Harvard of a series of vast halls which give a burlesque of college life is like the erection of crystal palaces when we need hotbeds.

Just as the key to improvement in our whole system of education lies in the removal of nonconductors between teacher and scholar, so the key to our university life lies in creating groups where special intellectual conductivity is provided for by segregation.

No sudden revolution in our system of university government is necessary or desirable. The reforms that creep in almost unnoticed are the important ones, for they show the tendency of the age. New and liberating influences can be set in motion without a ukase. The red tapes can be snipped severally as we come to see where they pinch. Each of them is an attempt to save somebody from a responsibility that should be thrown upon him. All regulations should be such that they can be easily relaxed in favor of exceptional talent in a student or exceptional intellectual power in a professor. Any one of our universities could quietly place a small group of scholars in charge of a house and grounds and allow them to live scholastically and socially. If such an experiment should succeed, it would become famous, and in ten years every clever boy in the country would be trying to get into the enclosure. The development of the humanities is subject to universal law. One must subserve Nature.

Made in the USA
Middletown, DE
21 September 2021

48710420R00062